Teenfluence Books

CAREER PLANNING for TEENS MADE SIMPLE

How to Unlock Your Potential for a Successful Career and Find a Path for a Healthy Working Environment

TEENFLUENCE YOUR PATH - YOUR POWER

OLIVE REDWOOD

Checked by Jennifer Smith, Careers Adviser

ISBN 978-3-949736-65-0 Paperback
ISBN 978-3-949736-66-7 E-book

First edition 2025
Part of the Teenfluence Series
lifecraftbooks.com

Your Free Gift

As a special thank-you for purchasing this book, I'm offering you access to an exclusive collection of FREE resources!

Instead of just one freebie, I've created a growing library of tools to support you on your career journey, including:

- **Cheat Sheets** to simplify the career exploration process.
- **Planners and Workbooks** to help you organize your goals and plans.
- **Additional Freebies,** which will be added regularly—so stay tuned!

To access these resources, **simply use the QR code** below:

Whether you're a teen ready to take on the world or a parent eager to guide your child toward success, these resources are designed to make career planning fun, easy, and achievable.

If you're ready to turn your dreams into plans and your plans into action, make sure to access your free library today.

Contents

How to Use This Book

Hey, Future World-Changer!

You're on the brink of something huge—figuring out your career path. It's like standing at the edge of a map, ready to discover new worlds, except these worlds are all about you and the future you're going to build.

Ready for the ride of your life? Before you set off, here's how to make the most of it:

- **Take Your Time:** No rush—your future isn't a sprint, it's a marathon. Digest each chapter at your own pace.
- **Get Interactive:** Each chapter has an exercise; jump into them. Scribble, doodle your thoughts—this book is your playground.
- **Reflect Deeply:** Use the reflection questions to dig deeper. They will help you explore your insights and dreams more thoroughly.
- **Be Honest:** This is a judgment-free zone. Be real with yourself; after all, it's your life you're mapping out.
- **Discuss and Share:** Talk about what you're discovering with people you trust. Sharing can open new doors and shine a light on paths you might not have noticed.

Keep an eye out for this symbol,
it means there's important information.

Questions in italics are for you to think about. Be honest with your answers and write them down in a notebook for future reference.

Actions or exercises for you to do will be highlighted and framed in gray.

What will you need?

- First up, a sturdy **notebook.** This will be your trusty sidekick, holding all your reflections, insights, and doodles. Go for a size that feels right to carry around but also gives you enough space to let your ideas flow.

- You'll need **pens**—and not just one. Grab a few in different colors to make your notes stand out, highlight important points, and even color-code your thoughts. Colors can be powerful memory aids, plus they make your pages look really cool.

- **Pencils** are great too, especially if you're sketching diagrams or charts, or just like the freedom to erase and rejig your thoughts. And don't forget a good eraser—because making mistakes is part of figuring stuff out.

- Some other handy tools might include **highlighters** to illuminate key ideas, **sticky notes** for those extra thoughts that need a place, and **page markers** to quickly zip back to important sections.

- Find a comfortable, **inspiring space to work.** Good lighting, a flat surface, and a splash of quiet can make all the difference.

You're the main character in this story, and every page is a step toward figuring out who you are and what you can become.

Welcome to Your Future!

Olive Redwood

Introduction

The journey toward your future career might seem a little intimidating. Where do you start? Which path do you take? But don't worry, it's not as scary as it seems.

I'm not here to hand you a career out of the blue. Instead, I'll give you the tools, the map, and the treasure chest—OK, not a real treasure chest but a metaphorical one filled with exercises, stories, advice, and reflections. You'll dig into what makes you tick, the things you rock at without even trying, and the values you stand for. You'll then learn how to transform them all into a career that doesn't just sound good but feels right too.

Here's how we do it:

- **Getting to Know You:** Take some time for a little self-discovery. Knowing your interests, your strengths, and your values will help you find the right paths.

- **Setting Goals:** Time to dream about where you'd like to see yourself in the future.

- **Checking Out the Scene:** So, once you've got a clearer picture of you, you're ready to explore what's out there. Dive into research, learn about different professions that match your passions and skills.

- **Getting There:** You've got your goals, now you need a roadmap. This could mean figuring out what classes to take, what experience you need, or even the people you should connect with.

- **Challenges:** You might come across some bumps in the road. These hurdles help you grow stronger and smarter.

- **Change is Cool:** Remember, this journey isn't carved in stone. As you grow, you might discover new interests, or the job scene might change. It's always okay to revisit your plan, make tweaks, or even change direction.

Throughout this book you'll hear from individuals who have overcome adversities, taken unexpected turns, and found success. These stories will provide insights, showing you that the path to career fulfillment isn't always a straight one but reassuring you that it is worth it.

Above all, this book is your guide—crafted with care to be informative, engaging, and relevant to you, the brilliant teens of today. It takes into account your unique viewpoints, aspirations, and uncertainties, providing you with tools, advice, and support.

The road to your future career is waiting.

Are you ready?
Turn the page, and let's get started.

Chapter 1
Self-Discovery

Life isn't about finding yourself.
Life is about creating yourself.

George Bernard Shaw

You're standing on the edge of a new adventure, like a map full of unknown places waiting for you to explore. That's your future—so many possibilities stretching out in front of you waiting for you to start. Now, imagine you've got a special tool in your hand, not a regular compass-which points north-but one which points inward to who you really are. This tool is self-discovery, and it can help you figure out what you want to do for work as you plan your career journey.

The teen years hold a secret power. They are the time where identity takes shape from new experiences. This period is critical for self-awareness because it's when you begin to distinguish your voice from the chorus around you. Your interests aren't just hobbies; they're direct indicators of potential career possibilities. Your skills are more than abilities; they can enable you to carve out your niche in the world. And your values? They ensure you stay true to what you believe in.

Interests: These are the subjects that catch your eye and hold your attention without effort. They're the activities you lose hours in because they ignite something inside you. Recognizing these passions is important as it will help you discover potential careers that won't just sustain you but also fulfill you.

Now, something to consider—you don't necessarily have to turn your main interests or passions into your career. Hobbies can simply be that—hobbies. Yet it can be helpful to identify what it is about these hobbies that you enjoy or find interesting. Find the essence of your hobbies—what makes them enjoyable or challenging—and look for ways that this essence could be applicable in a job or career path.

Skills: The talents and abilities you naturally possess or have honed over time—these are vital for getting access into the job market. They're what set you apart from others and enable you to contribute in unique ways. Identifying these skills will ensure you are ready to take on opportunities which arise.

Values: The principles and beliefs that anchor you and shape how you view work and life. They influence not just what career you choose but also how you engage with it. When your work aligns with your values, it resonates deeper, lasting longer and feeling more meaningful.

Getting to know yourself isn't something you can rush through—it's an adventure that deserves your attention and effort. When you really understand who you are, it's like finding the right pieces for a puzzle made just for you. So, start this journey of self-discovery with curiosity by your side and courage leading the way—because once you know yourself well, a world of opportunity will open up to you. You'll be able to see a future career which feels just right for you.

You know what? It's okay if you're not ready to pick a career yet. This book can help with that! It will help guide you to discover what you love, what you're good at—all at your own pace, there is no need to rush.

It's your journey. No stress, you've got this!

The Power of Self-Awareness

You find yourself in a room filled with mirrors, each reflecting not just your image but facets of your being you've never paused to examine. Self-awareness is like these mirrors, revealing **strengths** you can harness and **weaknesses** you can address, all of which shape the foundation of your career planning. It's not vanity to study your reflection here; it's strategy.

Self-awareness is more than just a buzzword; it's the conscious knowledge of one's own character, feelings, desires, and motivations. In the context of career planning, self-awareness helps you distinguish between fleeting interests and genuine passions, between a professed skill and a mastered one.

It's the tool that allows for the identification of careers that suit your abilities and also fulfill your aspirations.

Understanding who you are—what ignites your passion, what tasks you excel at, and where you falter—is the cornerstone of building a future that's authentically yours. A career that aligns with your inner self is more than a job; it's a calling that resonates with every step you take.

Consider the story of Maya, a high school junior whose love for storytelling was as vast as the ocean. She spent her evenings weaving tales, her words flowing onto pages. Her friends marveled at her narratives, but Maya saw it as just a hobby until she delved into self-awareness. She uncovered her strengths in communication and creativity and recognized that her passion could be her profession. Now, as a well-known author, Maya credits her fulfilling career to the mirror of self-awareness she realized as a teen.

Imagine Kevin, who always struggled with numbers and formulas but thrived on understanding people's emotions and motivations. Rather than forcing himself into an ill-fitting role in finance, self-awareness led him to psychology. Today, he helps others as a counselor. His career is built on the bedrock of his natural inclinations.

Then there's Sandra. From a young age she showed an affinity for organizing and planning—strengths that she recognized and others affirmed. Through self-awareness exercises, she discovered her knack for leadership and her passion for social causes. This combination of knowledge and passion led her to a fulfilling career managing nonprofit initiatives, where her strengths could shine, and her values were in harmony with her work.

Similarly, Mark understood early on that his strength lay in visual thinking, and his spatial intelligence was unmatched—traits he might have undervalued without self-awareness. By recognizing these, he pursued architecture, a field where he could leverage these strengths, leading to a gratifying career designing sustainable buildings.

But how do you increase self-awareness?

- Start by looking inward through **personality tests** that offer insights into how you think and interact with the world.

- Don't overlook the power of **feedback from others.** Sometimes those around you hold pieces of your mirror that you've yet to see. Teachers, mentors, friends—they all can provide valuable perspectives that help piece together the full picture of who you are.

- **Reflective exercises,** such as journaling or mindfulness practices, enable you to introspect and become attuned to your inner dialogues and desires.

- Engage in **varied experiences**—volunteer work, internships, clubs—that challenge different aspects of yourself. In action and reflection, you'll discover likes and dislikes that can help you understand what to aim for or avoid in a career.

- **AI-powered tools** like ChatGPT are designed to facilitate conversations and provide useful responses based on inputs. How cool is that? Say you want to explore careers better suited to your interests, skills, and qualifications, you can ask ChatGPT directly, and it will provide suggestions based on the details you've provided!

Remember, self-awareness isn't about fixing yourself; it's about knowing yourself, so when you stand at life's crossroads, you find it easier to choose the path which will be fulfilling for you.

The Heart of Career Satisfaction

You lean back in your chair, a notebook sprawled open in front of you, its blank pages mirroring the questions swirling in your mind.

What excites you?
What makes your heart beat faster?

These questions can help you to discover a career which won't feel like work because it's intertwined with what you love.

Personal interests are those pursuits that capture your imagination and refuse to let go. They are the activities you'd choose over and over, even if no one was watching. When these interests align with your career, each day dawns with possibility rather than monotony.

Take Leah, for instance, she grew up with her eyes glued to the stars, her nights spent tracing constellations and dreaming of distant galaxies. Her friends didn't understand her fascination with astronomy; they saw it as impractical. But Leah stayed true to her passion. Today, Dr. Leah is a renowned astronomer, contributing to our understanding of the universe. Her childhood interest is now the heartbeat of her career.

Eduardo's tale shows a similar journey. Immersed in the world of fashion and design from a young age, he often found himself sketching designs and following the latest trends. Despite social pressure to pursue a more 'traditional' career path, Eduardo honed his skills, attending a prestigious fashion school and, eventually, launching a successful clothing line that reflected his unique aesthetic. His story underscores career satisfaction built on the foundation of true interests.

To discern your own interests, consider immersing yourself in experiences outside the classroom. Here are some examples:

- **Internships** offer a taste of professional life in fields that pique your curiosity.
- **Volunteering** can expose you to different fields related to your passions while contributing to your communities.
- Joining **clubs or societies** can connect you with like-minded peers and mentors who can further fuel your passions.
- And never underestimate **hobbies,** they can often be transformed into career opportunities, with dedication and strategy.

Do you lose track of time when coding a new program?
Does organizing community events leave you buzzing with energy?

Write down some activities you take part in.
Think about how each activity makes you feel.

These are clues to where your interests lie.

But what about when outside voices try to drown out that inner call?

Peer pressure can steer you toward paths well-trodden but don't stay true to your core interests. Social expectations may box you into conventional roles that clash with your unique passions.

Keep yourself grounded by going back to what makes you really excited—those times when you're so into something that you don't even realize how much time has passed.

Skills and Talents

As you survey your interests and passions, remember that your skills and talents are the tools in your career toolkit.

Talents often present as innate abilities—those things you do effortlessly, the actions that come naturally to you, like a knack for understanding complex problems or an ear for musical nuances.

Skills, on the other hand, are abilities you've developed through learning and practice. Think of them as talents honed to precision through dedication—your piano playing getting richer with each hour of practice, your coding improving with every project completed.

Imagine a garden where talents are the seeds you've been given. These seeds might grow on their own to an extent, but skills are the result of nurturing these seeds—watering, weeding, and fertilizing them to reach their full potential. Your innate talent for storytelling becomes a skill when you study narrative structure and character development; your natural athleticism transforms into skill with coaching and regimented training.

These skills can totally change where your career goes. They can open up all sorts of opportunities for you and might help you find new paths you didn't even know were there.

To identify your current skills, start with assessments like skills inventories or aptitude tests that help map out your strengths and areas for growth. Seek feedback from teachers or mentors—those who have observed you in action and can provide insights into your capabilities.

- **Skills inventories** are like personal inventory checklists for your abilities. They help you tally the cool stuff you're good at—from mixing beats or coding websites to rallying your friends or solving complex puzzles. These inventories are about getting you to say, "Hey, I've got some serious skills!"

- **Aptitude tests** enable you to discover hidden talents. They're not about what you've learned in school, they're about the raw potential you've got packed in your brain.

Education plays a pivotal role in skill enhancement. Whether through formal schooling, online courses, or workshops, education equips you with the knowledge and practice needed to refine your talents into marketable skills.

As well as identifying and enhancing skills, it's important to apply them. Take Ana's story as an example. She identified her talent for negotiation during mock trials in her high school civics class. Realizing this could be more than just a school activity, she pursued internships in law firms over the summers. These experiences enhanced her natural talent, turning it into a robust skill set which enabled her to apply them to help her understand legal terminology, draft contracts, and mediate disputes. When Ana entered law school, she was steps ahead due to her developed skills. Now, as a successful attorney, Ana credits her career success to recognizing her innate talent early on and taking every opportunity to turn it into a finely tuned skill.

Practice is essential—it helps you remember what you've learned and gets you even better at it.

Just like how athletes train for hours to improve at their sport, or artists keep practicing making their work even more awesome, practicing what you're good at is super important.

So, as you wonder about where you want to go, think about what you're naturally good at. With some focus and commitment, you can turn those talents into skills that will help you stand out in whatever career path you choose.

Values

As you begin thinking seriously about what you want to do for work, your values are starting to point you in the direction of jobs that really feel right for you. These aren't just passing likes or dislikes but the big ideas that make you who you are. They are the non-negotiables, the parts of life and work that you think are super important—like maybe how much you value being creative, how excited you are about coming up with new ideas, or how committed you are to helping others.

Values should influence every aspect of your career choice, from the type of work you pursue to the environment in which you thrive, so that you can be happy in your line of work. They shape decisions about company culture—whether you align with a startup's risk-taking ethos or a nonprofit's humanitarian mission. Values also play a pivotal role in work-life balance, determining what sacrifices are acceptable and what compromises are too great.

Consider values such as integrity, innovation, social responsibility, or work-life balance.

Each of these plays a significant role in shaping the contours of one's career. A person who holds integrity in high regard may find great satisfaction in compliance or law, careers where upholding principles is a daily routine.

Conversely, innovation-driven individuals might gravitate toward start-up cultures or research and development roles where they can regularly push boundaries.

Sarah believed that family was the most important thing. She chose a career that offered flexibility over one with unpredictable hours, even if it meant a slower climb up the corporate ladder. Her choice ensured she could attend her children's soccer games and school plays—moments irreplaceable and priceless to her.

Jamal valued innovation above stability. He sought out companies that prioritized cutting-edge research and encouraged bold ideas. This led him to a tech startup where his contributions were instrumental in developing new software that changed the way people interacted with their devices.

To uncover your own values, begin with reflection questions.

What matters most to you?
When have you felt most fulfilled?
What causes do you believe in?

Discussions with mentors or trusted peers can also shed light on your values. These conversations show what is important to you through the words you use, the actions you've taken, or opinions you've given—often without realizing it.

Take stock of the times when **you've felt a strong sense of satisfaction** or purpose. Was it when volunteering at an animal shelter?

Or perhaps while working on a challenging project with a team? These instances are breadcrumbs leading back to your values.

It's important to know that your values can change as you grow up and go through different things. For example, when you're younger, you might really love having freedom and doing things on your own, but as you get older, you might start to crave being part of a community and working with others. Checking in with yourself regularly helps make sure that the job you're aiming for matches up with what you care about right now.

Values aren't just abstract concepts; they're the DNA of meaningful work. When your job lines up with what you truly believe in, you don't just like your job, you feel fulfilled and happy in your work, and that happiness spreads to everything else you do.

You're about to shape your own future based on what you've learned. Remember those moments when you really understood yourself. Your passions, talents, and values are more than just parts of who you are, they're what you can use to build a career that makes you happy and gives your life meaning.

Coming up in Chapter 2, we'll translate this self-knowledge into setting solid, actionable career goals.

Exercise

Personal Reflection Journaling

This worksheet for personal reflection journaling helps you to see what's going on in your head and heart. It's here for you to discover different aspects of what makes you, well, you.

This can enable you to uncover your real interests, figure out what you're good at, understand what matters most to you, and align all these insights with your future aspirations. Plus, it's going to give you a game plan to start making your dreams happen.

How to Use It

- **Exploring Interests:** Grab your favorite pen and jot down what really gets you pumped. Is it when you're playing the guitar, coding a new app, or maybe when you're planning an event with friends?

- **Assessing Skills:** Reflect on the things you just seem to get without much effort. Maybe you've got a knack for math, you're the peacemaker in your friend group, or you're the go-to person for building things.

- **Understanding Values:** Think about the moments you feel really proud or upset about something you hear in the news or see online. What's driving those feelings? Maybe equality is super important to you, or honesty.

- **Aligning Career Aspirations:** Dream a little here. If there were no limits, what would your perfect workday look like? Writing stories, teaching kids, designing buildings, or maybe running your own business?

- **Setting and Achieving Goals:** Break down your dreams into bite-sized pieces. Say you want to be a chef; a short-term goal might be to try cooking a new recipe once a week. A long-term goal could be to land a summer job at a local restaurant.

Just take it one question at a time. Don't stress about having all the answers right away. This is a process, kind of like building a playlist that fits all your moods. The more you put into it, the better it gets at helping you dance joyfully. Happy journaling!

Exploring Interests

What activities excite and energize me?

When do I feel most engaged and enthusiastic, and what am I doing during those times?

Assessing Skills

Which tasks come naturally to me, or what are others always asking me to help them with?

In which areas do I feel confident and competent?

Understanding Values

What principles help me decide what to do?

When I see what people or organizations are doing, which ones do I really connect with, and which ones make me feel uneasy?

Aligning Career Aspirations

When I envision my ideal workday, what am I doing, who am I interacting with, and what impact am I having? What does my physical working environment look like?

Setting and Achieving Goals

What are my short-term and long-term goals, and what small steps can I take this week and this month to move closer to achieving them?

Additional Notes

Chapter 2
Career Goals

You have to maintain a culture of transformation and stay true to your values.

Jeff Weiner

Welcome to the world of goal-setting. If you're wondering what this has to do with your career planning journey, let me assure you, it has everything to do with it. Goals guide us through unfamiliar places, helping us find our way.

Imagine you're on a road trip without a map or a GPS. You have no idea where you're going or how to get there. It's confusing and frustrating, right? That's what career planning can feel like without goals. Now imagine that same road trip, but this time you have a detailed map and clear directions. Suddenly, the journey doesn't seem so daunting anymore. You know exactly where you're going and how to get there.

So, let's discover the world of goal-setting—a world where dreams are broken down into actionable steps, where ambition meets strategy, and where career planning becomes less of an overwhelming task and more of an exciting journey.

Goal-Setting

You might be wondering why setting career goals is so important. Having clear, achievable, and well-defined career goals provide a sense of direction.

But the benefits of goal-setting don't stop there. Not only does it **give you direction,** but it also **fuels your motivation.** Each time you achieve a smaller milestone—a step toward your ultimate career goal—it feels like a victory.

This sense of achievement boosts your confidence and propels you forward, keeping your motivation alive.

Goals also **provide focus.** In the vast universe of career possibilities, it's easy to get overwhelmed. However, when you have specific goals in mind, it narrows down your focus, helping you concentrate on relevant opportunities and discard distractions. It makes the end goal feel more achievable when it's broken down into specific, smaller goals.

Goals **cultivate resilience.** Let's be honest, the journey to your dream career won't always be smooth-sailing. There will be setbacks and hurdles along the way. But when you have set goals that truly matter to you, they act as a beacon of hope in challenging times, fostering resilience and determination to keep going.

Now that we understand why setting career goals is essential, let's discover how to create them effectively.

- Formulating realistic and personally significant career goals begins with tapping into the **self-awareness** you've gained from the previous chapter. Remember those interests, skills, and values we talked about? They're an important part in shaping your career goals and can serve as a starting point for identifying potential career goals.

Consider these questions:

What careers align with your interests?
Which professions would allow you to leverage your skills?
How can your values guide your choice of industry or job role?

- It's crucial to ensure your goals are both **challenging and achievable.** Setting the bar too high can lead to frustration, while setting it too low may not provide the motivation you need to push forward. So, aim for a balance—set goals that require effort and growth but are within reach with determination and hard work.

- Make your goals **personally significant.** This isn't about what your parents, teachers, or friends think you should do. It's about what you want for your career and life. Remember, these are your goals, so they should reflect your aspirations, not someone else's.

Reflect on these strategies:

What career goal can you set today that aligns with your interests, leverages your skills, resonates with your values, and inspires you to strive forward?

The answer to this question will help you on your journey toward a fulfilling career.

SMART Goals

As you're discovering your journey in career planning, now's the time to get to know SMART goals. You may have come across this term before, but what does it mean in the context of your career aspirations?

SMART is an acronym that stands for Specific, Measurable, Achievable, Relevant, and Time-Bound. Each letter represents a critical aspect of effective goal-setting. Let's break it down together.

- **S stands for Specific.** In terms of your career goals, this means being clear and precise about what you want to achieve. Instead of saying, *"I want a good job,"* make it more specific: *"I want to become a software engineer at a tech startup."*

- **M is for Measurable.** You need to be able to track your progress. For instance, if your goal is to become a software engineer, a measurable milestone could be *"Complete a coding bootcamp"* or *"Build my own app."*

- **A signifies Achievable.** While it's great to dream big, it's also important to ground your goals in reality. If you're just starting out in coding, for example, aiming to become the lead engineer at Google within a year might be unrealistic. A more achievable goal may be to land an internship or entry-level position in the field within that time frame.

- **R stands for Relevant.** Your goals should align with your broader career aspirations and personal values. If you value work-life balance and creative freedom, becoming a freelance software developer might align better with those values than working for a large corporation.

- **T is for Time-Bound.** Setting a deadline for your goals creates a sense of urgency and keeps you motivated. Instead of saying, *"I want to learn to code,"* say, *"I want to complete a coding bootcamp by the end of the year."* This provides a clear time frame for achieving your goal.

Let's look at an example. Meet Alex, a high school senior with a passion for technology and problem-solving. After exploring various career paths, Alex decided to pursue software engineering. Here's how Alex set a SMART goal:

Specific:	*"I want to land an internship in software engineering at a local tech company."*
Measurable:	*"I will apply to at least five internships and aim to secure one by the end of the summer."*
Achievable:	*"I will complete an online coding bootcamp and work on personal projects to build my portfolio."*
Relevant:	*"This goal aligns with my long-term aspiration of becoming a software engineer and my interest in technology."*

Time-Bound: *"I aim to secure an internship by the end of August, giving me three months to prepare my applications and enhance my skills."*

By applying the SMART framework, Alex transformed a vague desire into a clear, actionable goal.

It's important to remember that sometimes things don't always go as planned. That's where **a backup plan** comes in handy. You can also use the SMART method to make that, too.

Let's create a backup plan for Alex. Suppose his ideal internship doesn't work out. A SMART backup goal could look like this:

Specific: *"If I don't secure an internship, I will aim to work on a complex software project that can enhance my coding skills and add to my portfolio."*

Measurable: *"I will dedicate at least 20 hours a week to this project and aim to complete it by the end of summer."*

Achievable: *"With the skills I've gained from the coding bootcamp and personal projects, I'm confident that I can accomplish this."*

Relevant: *"Working on this project will supplement my learning, hone my programming skills, and contribute to my long-term career goal."*

Time-Bound: *"I aim to complete the project by the end of August."*

See, with a backup SMART goal, Alex still has a concrete plan to build his software engineering skills, even if the initial internship plan doesn't pan out. It's like a safety net that keeps you moving forward on your career path, no matter what!

Now it's your turn.

What SMART career goal and backup plan can you set today?

Your Passion and Long-Term Plans

As you venture deeper into your career planning journey, you may start to notice a pattern. All the self-discovery, goal setting, and planning you've been doing? They all circle back to one crucial point: **You.** Your aspirations, your interests, and your long-term plans are the lifeblood of your career goals. Without them, your goals are just empty shells, devoid of personal significance and motivation. Take a moment to consider these questions:

What are your deepest desires?
What life do you envisage for yourself?
Do your career goals reflect these personal aspirations?

If not, it's time to rethink them. Because when your career goals resonate with your personal dreams, they lead you to the life you desire.

But how do you infuse personal aspirations into career goals? It starts by **assessing your passions.** Not just fleeting interests or hobbies but passions that ignite a fire within you—those that make you lose track of time or give you a sense of fulfillment.

Take a pen and paper or open a new document on your device. Write down answers to these questions.

What activities energize me?
What topics do I find endlessly fascinating?
What tasks do I look forward to doing?
What causes am I passionate about?

Don't rush this process. Take your time. Reflect deeply.

And remember, there are no right or wrong answers here—only truths that will guide you toward more meaningful career goals.

Next comes **long-term planning.** Setting career goals is like planning a road trip to your dream destination—your ultimate career vision. And like any road trip, there will be detours and unexpected stops along the way. Your interests may evolve over time. New opportunities may emerge that weren't on the horizon when you started out. Life might throw curveballs that require you to adjust your course. That's why flexibility is crucial in long-term career planning.

Think about your ultimate career vision. What short-term actions do you need to take to move closer to that long-term aim? This strategy allows you to break down a seemingly daunting journey into manageable steps, each moving you closer to your career dream.

Your career is more than just a job or a profession—it's an integral part of your life. Make sure it reflects who you are and the life you aspire to live. Because, at the end of the day, your career should not just be something you do—it should be a testament to who you are.

The 4Ps

Alright, let's gather around for a cool concept that's straight-up powerful when it comes to making decisions and taking charge of your future: the 4Ps model. This is a practical strategy to break down and tackle just about anything—from homework to major life choices like career planning.

The **4Ps** stand for **Picture, Plan, Proceed,** and **Perfect.** These steps help you zoom out for an overview and then zoom in to nail the details. It's a cycle that you can loop back through as needed, making it perfect for refining ideas and reaching your goals.

- **Picture.** Start with a broad view of what you want. This could be something big like becoming a software developer, or something more immediate like acing your biology exam. Create a clear mental image in your mind. Ask yourself: *What's my ultimate goal? What does achieving this look like? Who do I know that has accomplished this?* Visualizing the end result gives you something tangible to aim for.

- **Plan.** Alright, you've got your picture, now how do you make it real? It's planning time. This involves brainstorming the steps you need to take, resources you'll need, and the timeline for getting there. Do you need to learn a coding language? Should you talk to a career counselor or a biologist for insights? Break down your big goal into smaller, actionable steps. This way, you're not trying to leap to the Moon in one go—you're building a ladder, rung by rung.

- **Proceed.** Got your plan? Let's roll. This is where you start taking action, following your plan step by step. It's all about momentum now. Remember, progress is progress, no matter how slow. Hit your study schedule, sign up for that coding class, or start your science project. Sometimes things go sideways, and that's okay—it's part of the journey.

- **Perfect.** As you move along, you'll learn and grow, and so will your approach. Perfecting is about tweaking things to make them better. After some time coding, maybe you find out you're more interested in game development, or your science project sparks a passion for environmental conservation. Reflect on your progress, get feedback, and adjust your plan as you learn more about your goals and yourself.

The beauty of the 4Ps is their flexibility. You can apply this method to short-term projects or lifelong dreams. It's about vision and adaptability, starting with a grand Picture, crafting a Plan, taking action to Proceed, and refining it all to Perfect your approach.

So, whether you're selecting a college, planning your career, or just trying to nail a kickflip on your skateboard, the 4Ps are a handy way to bring your A-game.

Your career should be a testament to who you are. Let it reflect your passions and values. Let it lead you to the life you yearn for. As well as planning your career, you're shaping your future. So go ahead and set those SMART career goals and 4Ps—and ensure they are true to who you are and what you aspire to become.

As Chapter 3 approaches, we take the foundation of self-knowledge and defined goals to the next level—exploring a diverse array of career options to find your best fit.

Exercise

SMART Goal-Setting Worksheet

This worksheet will guide you through crafting SMART career goals. SMART goals are Specific, Measurable, Achievable, Relevant, and Time-Bound.

By filling out this worksheet, you'll transform broad career aspirations into focused plans of action. Define at least one short-term goal (something you can achieve within the next year) and one long-term goal (something to work toward in the next five years or beyond).

How to Use It

- **Mentally Warm Up:** Think about what fires you up, the career milestones you're eager to hit or the skills you're itching to master.
- **Get SMART:** For each goal, you're going to get laser-specific with the SMART criteria.
- **Craft Your Goals:** Start with one short-term goal—something that's just around the corner, within a year's reach. Then, map out a long-term goal for the big dream, the 'where do you see yourself in five years' kind of stuff.
- **Reflect:** Spot potential challenges and think about how you could knock them down. Consider how these goals mirror what's important to you personally.
- **Review and Revise:** Rome wasn't built in a day, and neither are careers. Check back on your goals now and then. Tweak them as you grow and as life throws curveballs your way.

Goal 1: Short-Term

Specific: What exactly do you want to accomplish in detail? Who is involved? Where will it happen? Why do you want to achieve this goal?

Measurable: How will you track your progress and measure success? What metrics or milestones will you use?

Achievable: Is the goal realistic with effort? Do you have the resources you need or can you obtain them?

Relevant: Why is this goal significant to your career plans? Does it align with your long-term aspirations?

Time-Bound: When will you achieve this goal? Set a deadline.

Goal 2: Long-Term

Specific: What are your big-picture career goals? Consider positions you want to reach, expertise you want to develop, or the impact you wish to have.

Measurable: Identify how you'll measure the success over the long-term. What are the long-term indicators of success?

Achievable: How can you achieve this goal over the long-term? What skills or resources are needed, and how will you acquire them?

Relevant: How does this goal fit into your desired career path and personal growth?

Time-Bound: When do you expect to reach this goal? While it's long-term, establishing a target year can provide direction.

Reflection Section

What challenges do you anticipate in achieving these goals, and how can you prepare to overcome them?

How do these goals reflect your personal values and interests?

Remember to review your goals periodically and adjust them as needed. Life changes, and so might your interests and opportunities.

Additional Notes

Chapter 3
Different Career Paths

Passion is what gives meaning to our lives.
It's what allows us to achieve success beyond our wildest imagination.
Try to find a career path that you have a passion for.

Henry Samueli

Thinking about all the different jobs out there can feel like exploring a huge, unknown ocean. There are so many possibilities—different jobs, industries, and roles, each with its own set of things you need to do, what you'll get, and what could be tough about it. It's a lot to take in—how do you even start figuring it all out? That's where career exploration comes in.

Career exploration is more than just listing different jobs. It explores and helps you really understand what each job is about—what you'll do, what's expected, and what you'll get in return. It's discovering the layers of different industries and roles to see how they work. But, most importantly, it's about matching up what you learn with what you already know about yourself.

This chapter will provide you with methods and strategies to **explore and evaluate various career options.** You'll learn how to research different industries, job roles, and professions, and how to dissect them to understand their core components.

You'll learn about **informational interviews**—a tool that allows you to tap into the knowledge of professionals in your fields of interest.

You'll also discover **job shadowing**—another valuable tool that offers a sneak peek into the day-to-day workings of a profession. Picture yourself observing a professional in action, seeing firsthand what a day in their life looks like. Imagine having a candid conversation with someone who's walking the path you're considering, who can share insights about the realities of the job that no website or brochure can provide.

Finally, this chapter will underscore the importance of understanding the **education, training, and skills required** for different careers. Exploring careers helps you find what interests you and how you can go about succeeding in a specific field.

Career exploration is a journey. So set sail, navigate the vast sea of possibilities, and discover what lies beyond the horizon.

Researching Different Industries, Job Roles, and Professions

As you think about what you want to do with your future, researching different industries, job roles, and professions is a good step to take. You can dig deep, gather facts, and see firsthand what each job is really like. This will make sure you know enough to make smart choices about where you're headed.

The importance of thorough industry research cannot be overstated. Each industry, job role, and profession have their own unique features—their own set of requirements, challenges, and rewards. By understanding these facets, you position yourself to choose a career path that sits right with your interests, skills, values, and aspirations.

So, how do you go about conducting this research? The answer lies in a systematic approach.

- Start with online databases like the **U.S. Occupational Outlook Handbook**—a treasure trove of information on hundreds of occupations. Here, you'll find details about the nature of work, education requirements, job outlooks, salaries, and more.

But don't stop there.

- Research **industry-specific publications and professional association resources.** These can provide deeper insights into current trends, emerging opportunities, and industry challenges. Reading these resources can give you a sense of the dynamics of each industry—something that can be invaluable when making career decisions.

- Consider constructing an **industry and profession matrix**—a tool that can help you compare different career paths.

Start by listing industries or professions that interest you in the first column. In subsequent columns, jot down key factors such as educational requirements, typical job duties, potential salary ranges, job outlooks, and anything else that seems relevant.

As you fill in this matrix with information from your research, patterns may begin to emerge. Certain industries or professions might align more closely with your interests or skills. Others might offer growth opportunities that excite you.

Understanding the vast array of sectors, roles, and career prospects can be a **game-changer.** It can open your eyes to opportunities you might not have considered. It can give you a sense of direction, a sense of purpose. And, most importantly, it can empower you to make informed decisions about your future.

Social media platforms, from Instagram to LinkedIn, are powerful too and can open windows into various career paths and job roles that might not otherwise be visible.

It's crucial to remember that these platforms often only showcase a selected and polished version of reality and may not provide a comprehensive picture of a particular career.

While a curated Instagram feed might make a job look glamorous and rewarding, it may not reveal the less glamorous aspects—such as the long hours, hard work, and dedication required to qualify for and excel in that role. A YouTube vlog could give you an impression of an exciting day at work but might miss out on the mundane tasks or stressful moments that are also part of the job.

Don't let this discourage you from using social media as a resource in your career exploration journey. These platforms can indeed be fantastic **sources of inspiration** and provide valuable insights. The key is using social media as a complement to other resources, not the sole source of your information.

Researching career paths should not just rely on perceiving the 'highlight reel' on social media. Make a point to **dig deeper.** Use professional networking sites, career planning resources, and firsthand experiences. Speak with professionals in the field, attend career fairs, or seek out internships. These activities will give you a more complete and realistic picture of what a career entails.

This process is not about finding the 'perfect' career right off the bat. It's about **exploration and discovery.** It's about learning and growing. So, enjoy—immerse yourself in research, fill in your matrix, and see what insights emerge.

Non-Traditional Career Path

In your vibrant teenage years, when you're mapping out career paths, it can feel like they're full of opportunities which are there for the taking. Let's spice up your thinking with something cool—non-traditional careers.

So, what exactly are these?

Basically, non-traditional careers are jobs that **break away from what we usually think** are for boys or girls, rich or poor, or a specific race or ethnicity.

Consider a guy who's a preschool teacher. Teaching has often been seen as a job mainly for women, but why should that be the norm? Education is such an important field, full of opportunities to shape young minds and make a difference—ideal for anyone who's passionate about helping kids learn, regardless of their gender.

How about considering a teenager from a public school who dreams of becoming a politician? Society often assumes that politicians originate from private schools, but why should this be the expectation? Politics is about leadership, making a difference, and serving the people—perfect for anyone motivated and dedicated to making positive changes, no matter their educational background or wealth.

Think about a female scientist—someone breaking into a field that's mostly been for guys. But science isn't about whether you're a boy or a girl. It's about asking questions and being creative, and both men and women can do that. If you're into figuring out how the world works, there are labs everywhere waiting for your smart and cool ideas, no matter who you are.

So, why consider stepping into these non-traditional roles?

- **Personal satisfaction.** If you love something, nothing else should matter. Not your gender, not your social background, not your race.

- **Diverse perspectives.** A workplace with people from different backgrounds can come up with so many exciting ideas! It's because everyone brings something unique to the table.

However, going non-traditional could also mean you've got some trailblazing to do. It might require some thick skin as you dismantle stereotypes and prove doubters wrong. But hey, isn't that a challenge worth accepting? It's you versus outdated norms. And while there could be bumps along this less-trodden path, the rewards—breaking barriers, personal growth, making a difference—make the journey worthwhile.

Here you can find some examples why a non-traditional career path could be cool:

- **STEM Fields (Science, Technology, Engineering, Mathematics):** Women in STEM fields are growing in numbers but remain underrepresented, especially in engineering and information technology.

- **Politics:** You don't have to go to a private school to become a politician. Even a regular pupil attending a public school can gear up for this.

- **Nursing:** Male nurses are becoming more common, but the field of nursing is still predominantly women. Men in nursing bring valuable perspectives and help normalize the presence of male caregivers.

- **Law Enforcement:** From police officers to FBI agents, women in law enforcement contribute to a balanced and comprehensive approach to public safety and investigative work.

- **Tech Industry:** Anyone can develop the next big tech thing, can code, innovate, and lead, too, no matter your ethnicity, gender identity, or education.

- **Elementary Education:** Particularly at the kindergarten and elementary levels, there are fewer male teachers. Men in these roles can serve as important role models and mentors to young children.

Informational Interviews and Job Shadowing

Think of informational interviews as your opportunity to discover the reality of a specific job. They're full of useful info that can help you understand different careers better. You get to see what it's really like to do different jobs, which helps you figure out if they match up with what you're into, what you're good at, and what you dream of doing.

- **Informational interviews** are not job interviews but rather conversations where you're the interviewer. Imagine sitting across from a professional in your field of interest, peppering them with questions about their career journey, the nature of their work, and their industry insights. You can unlock a vault of real-world knowledge that can guide your career decisions.

  To embark on this quest, start by identifying professionals in the fields that interest you. They could be alumni from your school, speakers at industry events, or even professionals you find on LinkedIn. Reach out to them with a polite and concise email expressing your interest in learning about their career path and requesting a brief informational interview.

  Prepare for these interviews by researching the individual's background and industry. Create a list of meaningful questions that delve into the specifics of their job, their day-to-day tasks, their career progression, and their views on industry trends. Think about yourself and if there's something specific you'd like to know.

Check out Appendix 1, where you can find 10 meaningful questions which could help you with the interviews.

This is your chance to learn from someone who's walking the path you're considering—so don't shy away from asking about challenges they've faced or what they find most rewarding about their work.

- **Job shadowing** is another invaluable tool in your career exploration toolbox. It allows you to step into the shoes of a professional for a day or two—to observe firsthand what a day in their life looks like. This immersive experience can give you an unfiltered glimpse into the practical aspects of different jobs.

  Arranging job shadowing experiences might require some persistence, and an essential part of reaching out is presenting yourself professionally through a cover letter. When contacting professionals or human resources departments in your field of interest, attach a well-crafted cover letter to your request that expresses your desire to learn through observation. This cover letter is your chance to make a good first impression and should convey your enthusiasm and professionalism clearly. A thoughtful cover letter not only serves as a formal introduction but also showcases your communication skills and sets the tone for the experience you wish to gain.

Check out Appendix 2, where you can find the importance and structure of a cover letter.

Once arranged, make sure to clarify expectations—understand what you'll be allowed to observe and how you should conduct yourself.

As you shadow, be a keen observer. Note the interactions, the tasks, the environment, and the pace of work. Keep a **shadowing diary** where you jot down your observations, impressions, and any questions that arise. This record will be a valuable resource when you reflect on your experience later.

Imagine being a fly on the wall in a bustling architectural firm, watching as blueprints transform into three-dimensional models. Or observing a busy day in a medical clinic, witnessing the impact healthcare professionals have on their patients' lives. These experiences can bring career paths to life more than a description or picture in a leaflet can.

Incorporating informational interviews and job shadowing experiences into your career exploration journey can add depth to your understanding of various professions. They allow you to tap into real-world insights that can inform your career decisions.

Understanding the Education, Training, and Skills Required for Different Careers

An important facet emerges when exploring careers—the education, training, and skills required for that role. Just as a builder needs the right tools to construct a house, you need the right education and skills to build your career.

Understanding the **educational pathways** for your potential career is crucial. These pathways are as diverse as the careers themselves.

- For some, a traditional **four-year college degree** might be the way forward. Careers in fields like engineering, medicine, or law typically require this route. However, a university degree is not the only pathway.

- **Vocational schools** offer specialized training for careers in industries like healthcare or technology. These programs often take less time than a traditional degree and focus on equipping you with practical skills for specific jobs.

- **Apprenticeships** present another valuable avenue. Imagine learning a trade like carpentry or electrical work not just in a classroom but on the job, under the guidance of an experienced professional. These programs combine instruction with hands-on experience—a powerful combination that can pave the way to a rewarding career.

- And let's not forget **certifications**—valuable credentials that can boost your employability in fields like IT or project management. Certifications demonstrate your expertise and commitment to professional development, which employers value.

Each of these educational pathways offers unique benefits. Research the educational requirements of your potential careers—understand what qualifications they demand and consider how you can acquire them.

Next comes **skills analysis**—a process of mapping the skills required for your targeted careers against your current competencies. This exercise can help you identify any gaps and create a plan to fill them.

Start by listing the key skills needed for your potential careers—you can find this information through job descriptions or occupational databases. Next, assess your current skill set.

What strengths do you already possess?
Where could you improve?

Once you've identified any gaps, consider how you can develop these skills.

Perhaps you need to:

- take a course
- seek a mentor
- gain some practical experience through internships or volunteering

Finally, **strategic planning** is essential in prioritizing your education and skill-building efforts. With your career goals in mind, consider the most effective route to prepare yourself for your chosen field.

What strengths do you already possess?
Where could you improve?

Remember, strategic planning shouldn't be rigid—it needs to be flexible so that it can adapt to changing circumstances and opportunities. It needs to equip you with the tools needed to build the career that aligns with your interests, skills, values, and aspirations.

Success Stories

Lots of successful people have interesting careers that take them all over the place. What connects their stories isn't a straight line from Point A to Point B, but a bunch of choices, experiences, and sometimes the ability to bounce back from mistakes and unexpected turns.

Take, for example, **Steve Jobs,** whose iconic journey with Apple began in a garage and was anything but smooth. Jobs was actually fired from the company he founded in his early thirties, an event he later described as liberating and crucial to his subsequent success. Embracing creativity and innovation, he founded NeXT and purchased Pixar, eventually returning to Apple to lead it to become one of the world's most valuable companies.

Then there's **Oprah Winfrey,** who faced a challenging upbringing and early career setbacks in the media industry. Undeterred, she went on to host her own talk show, which transformed into a media and business empire, with Winfrey herself becoming a symbol of perseverance, empathy, and success.

Similarly, **J. K. Rowling's** story is a testament to transforming setbacks into steppingstones. As a single mother living on welfare, Rowling wrote the first Harry Potter book in cafes, only to be rejected by multiple publishers. When finally published, her work skyrocketed her to the pinnacle of literary stardom, establishing a global entertainment franchise.

In the realm of science, a figure like **Marie Curie** stands out. Curie persevered in her field at a time when women were rarely accepted in scientific communities. Her groundbreaking work in radioactivity (a term she coined) earned her two Nobel Prizes and paved the way for future innovations in medicine and physics.

Let's take a look at **Serena Williams,** one of the greatest tennis players of all time. With numerous Grand Slam titles to her name, she has also become a successful entrepreneur and advocate for gender equality in sports.

Or **LeBron James.** He is a professional basketball player widely regarded as one of the greatest athletes of all time. He has won multiple NBA championships and MVP awards, using his platform to advocate for social justice and education initiatives.

Another inspiring journey is that of **Taylor Swift,** one of the world's leading music artists. Shaping her destiny right from her early teens, she had a clear vision: to become a successful country music artist. Her raw talent and relentless hard work led to her signing a record deal at only 15. She then swiftly transitioned from a promising country artist to a global pop sensation. Persisting in the face of challenges and evolving her music over the years, Swift's journey goes to show that dedication, authenticity, and adaptability can indeed strike the right chord to success.

The journeys of these people show that reaching big goals often means taking risks, dealing with failures, and never giving up—even when things get tough. Whether it's coming up with new ideas, working super hard, or pushing past obstacles, their career paths show what you can do with determination and big dreams. Each story reminds us of something important: success isn't about never failing; it's about never giving up on what you love and want to achieve.

Again, this journey is not a sprint—it's a marathon. Career exploration is an ongoing process that evolves as you grow and gain more life experience. It's about being proactive: seeking out information, asking questions, gaining experience, and constantly reflecting on what you learn. But more than anything else, career exploration is about being open—open to various opportunities, open to unexpected paths, open to change.

Pivoting into Chapter 4, we'll be arming ourselves with decision-making skills. Guided by your enhanced understanding of potential career paths, we'll be making informed choices, and strategically moving toward your chosen profession.

Exercise

Educational Pathways Research Worksheet

Educational pathways research involves investigating all the educational qualifications, courses, training programs, and learning opportunities that can lead you to your chosen career. It's essential for understanding what steps you need to take educationally to prepare for your future profession.

As a teenager, you may be aware of your interests and potential career fields but less clear about how to get there. This research will help you map out the educational journey you must undertake to reach your professional goals.

How to Use It

- Decide on a career (or a few careers) you're interested in based on your previous reflection and exploration.
- Research each career to find out what kind of education, training, and skills are typically required.
- Use this worksheet to organize the information you gather. It will help you visualize and plan your potential educational route.

Tips for Successful Research

- Start with broad searches on career and education websites, then narrow down to specific programs or institutions.

- Reach out directly to educational institutions for more detailed information or to request brochures.
- Consider the employment rates and career outcomes of graduates from the programs you're interested in.
- Don't hesitate to contact professionals already in the field to ask for advice on the best educational paths to take.

Career Choice 1:

____

Typical Degree(s) or Certification(s) Required:
List the degrees or certifications commonly associated with entering this career.

Vocational Training or Apprenticeships Available:
Identify if there are specific vocational or on-the-job training opportunities that are recommended or required.

Colleges/Universities Offering Relevant Programs:
Name the academic institutions that offer the educational pathways you're interested in and any specializations they are known for. Also list what entry requirements they have.

Duration and Cost:

Estimate the duration of the educational pathway (how long it takes to complete the training or degree) and the potential costs involved.

Skills and Experiences Gained:

Briefly describe the skills and experiences that you will acquire during the educational process.

Repeat the same structure as above for each additional career choice you're exploring.

Reflection Section

Comparative Insights:

What similarities and differences do you see in the educational pathways for the careers you're interested in?

Personal Considerations:

How do the duration, cost, and location of these educational opportunities fit with your personal circumstances and goals?

Next Steps:

Based on your research, what are the immediate next steps you can take? (e.g., speaking with a school counselor, attending a college open day, arranging a campus tour, etc.)

Remember, education is a personal journey and what works well for one person might not be ideal for another. Use this research as a guide, but always factor in your individual circumstances, aspirations, and values when making decisions about your future education.

Additional Notes

Chapter 4
Career Decisions

A good decision is based on knowledge and not on numbers.

Plato

Making well-informed, realistic decisions can be hard for everyone. The path may seem challenging, but each turn brings you closer to your goal, keep going.

Decisions, big and small, are part of our daily lives. They may seem daunting at times, but if you break them down into smaller steps, they become more manageable.

1. **Identify that a Decision Needs to be Made:** Realize when you're faced with a choice. Do you need to make a decision now or can it wait?

2. **Gather Information:** Do you have all the facts you need to make an informed decision? If not, do some research. Find out more about your choices.

3. **Consider Your Options:** Use your research to weigh your options. Reflect on what matters to you the most.

4. **Make Your Decision:** Pick the option that aligns best with what you want or what you believe is right.

5. **Review Your Decision:** Reflect on the decision you made. Is it working out how you expected? If not, what can you learn from that?

Let's use a simple example: choosing a college major.

1. You need to decide on a major—a significant decision that affects your future career path (you've identified a decision that needs to be made).

2. Look into different fields of study. Research job prospects, future earnings, and the subjects that interest you. Attend college fairs, speak to professionals in the field, and engage with college advisers (gather information).

3. Reflect on the information gathered. Which fields align with your skills and interests? Consider your goals. Do you prioritize a high earning potential, job security, doing something you're passionate about, or a combination of factors? (Consider options.)

4. Choose the major that best fits with your aspirations, interests, and the lifestyle you'd like for your future (make decision).

5. As you begin your studies, evaluate your choice. Do you enjoy your courses? Do they motivate you? Are they helping you progress toward your career goals? It's okay to realize that something else might suit you better. Many students change their major as they grow and learn more about themselves and their goals (review decision).

See? Making a decision doesn't have to be overwhelming. Just remember, in career planning, like in daily life, it's normal not to get it perfectly right every time. What matters is to learn from your experiences and adjust as necessary.

Conducting Research on Potential Career Paths

Research is important, but it's only half the story. The other half is **thinking deeply about yourself**—asking tough questions and being honest with yourself.

Does this job match what you believe in?
Will it help you reach your goals?
Can you see yourself really enjoying it and doing well?

Conducting all this research and thinking about what you really want can feel like a big task. It takes time, effort, and being honest with yourself. But it's totally worth it—it's **investing in yourself and your future.** When you make smart choices now, you're steering your career toward something that brings success and also makes you happy.

Imagine yourself as a detective on a mission. Your task? To uncover the secrets of various career paths, to scrutinize their details, and to assess their fit for you. The clues are scattered across a myriad of resources, waiting to be discovered, analyzed, and understood. This is the essence of thorough research. Begin by asking yourself what you're looking for.

Do you crave the thrill of crunching numbers
in a bustling financial firm?
Does the idea of innovating technology
in a cutting-edge software company pique your interest?
Have you ever dreamed of saving lives
in a hospital or shaping minds in a classroom?

The world of careers is vast and diverse, and each path holds unique opportunities, challenges, and rewards. Now that you have a rough idea of your interests, it's time to look deeper. Begin by exploring the industry as a whole.

What trends are shaping its future?
What roles are emerging as crucial players?
How has the industry evolved over time?

Seek out reliable sources like the U.S. Occupational Outlook Handbook or industry-specific publications for these insights.

Once you've picked an industry you're interested in, it's time to focus on the actual jobs within it. Check out job listings to see what each role involves. Look closely at what they ask for.

Do you need certain degrees or certificates?
What skills and experience are they looking for?

Don't forget to look at the numbers: **salary trends, employment growth rates, and job stability.** While these shouldn't be your only deciding factors, they're important to be aware of.

Choose a career field that interests you.
Over the next week, dedicate some time each day to researching this field.
Start broad—explore the industry, its trends, and its key roles.
Then narrow down your focus to specific job roles.
Look at their requirements, their tasks, their salaries.
Take notes as you go along—you'll need them in the coming chapters.

Remember, detective, every piece of information is a clue, every clue brings you closer to your goal. So put on your detective hat and explore the exciting world of career research.

Personal Strengths, Weaknesses, and Preferences

Now let's turn the lens inward and examine your own strengths, weaknesses, and preferences. Just as a puzzle piece must fit perfectly into its spot, your personal attributes must align with your career choices.

- Think of your **strengths** as your superpowers—the unique abilities that set you apart from others. These could be hard skills like proficiency in a foreign language or coding, or soft skills like excellent communication or problem-solving. Identifying these strengths can help you find careers that use and develop them.

- Now, let's talk about **weaknesses**—areas where you may need improvement. Don't shy away from these; instead, see them as opportunities for growth. Perhaps you struggle with public speaking or find it challenging to work under pressure. By identifying these weaknesses, you can seek careers that challenge you to improve them or choose paths where they're less likely to hold you back.

- Finally, consider your **preferences**—the kind of work environment you thrive in, the values you hold dear, and the work style that suits you best. Your preferences can greatly influence your job satisfaction and performance.

Are you a self-starter who prefers working independently or do you thrive in collaborative environments?
Do you enjoy fast-paced work or prefer a more relaxed pace?

Now that we've covered what to look for, let's discuss how to find it. As we mentioned earlier, self-assessment tools and personality tests can provide valuable insights into your strengths, weaknesses, and preferences. Reputable tools like the Myers-Briggs Type Indicator (MBTI) or the StrengthsFinder can reveal aspects of your personality that directly impact your career choices.

Check out Appendix 3, where you can find out more about personality tests.

Do you remember Sarah? She was unsure about her career path until she took the MBTI test. The results revealed she was an ENFP (Extroverted, Intuitive, Feeling, and Perceiving)—a warm, enthusiastic person who loves helping others realize their potential. This insight led her to consider careers in counseling and human resources.

It's your turn now.

Choose a self-assessment tool or personality test and take it. Once you have the results, reflect on them.

Do they resonate with you?
How do they align with your career interests?

Take out a piece of paper. Draw a table with three columns: Strengths, Weaknesses, Preferences. Under each column, list your top five attributes based on your self-assessment results and personal introspection.

Next, pull out the notes from your career research. Start mapping your attributes to these careers.

Which careers best suit your strengths?
Which ones offer opportunities to improve your weaknesses?
Which ones match your preferences?

Finally, ponder over these reflective questions:

What do these insights reveal about your ideal career?
How can you leverage your strengths and improve your weaknesses to succeed in this career?

How can your preferences shape your work style in this career?

There are no right or wrong answers—only insights that bring you closer to making informed career decisions.

Core Values

The job you pick is a big part of your life. It will affect your growth in work but also how happy and fulfilled you feel in life overall. As I've said several times, it's important that you choose something that **fits with what you want** in the future and **what matters to you.**

Imagine your career as a ship sailing toward the horizon of your aspirations. Your values are the compass guiding this ship, ensuring it stays on course. When your career aligns with your aspirations and values, the journey is smooth and satisfying. But when there's misalignment, you may find yourself adrift in a sea of dissatisfaction and unfulfillment.

So how do you ensure alignment?

The answer lies in **values-based decision-making**—a process that involves weighing career options against your personal values and long-term aspirations.

Start by listing your **core values**—those principles that guide your actions and decisions. They could be anything from integrity and honesty to creativity and ambition. Next, list your long-term aspirations—the milestones you wish to achieve in life.

Now, consider each career option in light of these values and aspirations.

Does this career align with your core values?
Will it enable you to fulfill your long-term aspirations?
How will this career impact your personal life—your relationships, mental health, physical well-being?

You can make informed career decisions by considering the alignment of your choices with your values and aspirations. Take some time this week to reflect on your values, aspirations, and potential career paths. Ask yourself hard questions and seek honest answers.

Go With the Flow

Now that we have explored strategies for your career planning, I would like to introduce you to an interesting career planning theory, **Planned Happenstance.**

Have you ever heard the phrase "Go with the flow"? When it comes to career planning, there's a theory that suggests this might be one of the best strategies you can adopt. It's called Planned Happenstance, and it was developed by Prof. John Krumboltz from Stanford University. This theory is all about **the unexpected opportunities that life throws at us and how we can make the most of them.**

Planned Happenstance is the idea that you don't have to have everything figured out about your career from the start. Instead, it encourages you to **remain open** to new experiences and unexpected opportunities that can lead to exciting career paths. It's a mix of being prepared and being open to change, allowing unplanned events to positively influence your career journey.

Here are the key components of the theory:

- **Curiosity:** Always be curious. Ask questions, explore different subjects, and be willing to learn about things that catch your interest. This can lead you to discover passions you didn't even know you had.

- **Persistence:** Sometimes things don't go as planned. Don't get discouraged by setbacks. Keep trying and adapting to new situations.

- **Flexibility:** Be ready to change your plans when new opportunities arise. Life is unpredictable, and the ability to adapt is crucial.

- **Optimism:** Believe that unexpected events can be opportunities rather than obstacles. A positive outlook can help you see the potential in unplanned situations.

- **Risk-Taking:** Don't be afraid to step out of your comfort zone. Taking risks can lead to new experiences and opportunities that you wouldn't have encountered otherwise.

Imagine you're in high school and you're not sure what you want to do after you graduate. You might have some interests, but no clear career path. Planned Happenstance suggests that instead of stressing about making the perfect choice now, you should focus on exploring your interests and staying open to new possibilities. Here's how you can apply it:

- **Explore Broadly:** Take a variety of classes and engage in different extracurricular activities. You might discover a passion for something unexpected, like coding in a computer science class or creative writing in an English class.

- **Network:** Talk to people in different careers. Attend career fairs, join clubs, or even volunteer. Meeting people from various fields can open doors to opportunities you hadn't considered.

- **Stay Open-Minded:** Maybe you get a part-time job in a cafe and discover you love interacting with people and managing tasks. This experience might steer you toward a career in hospitality or business management, fields you hadn't thought about before.

- **Be Prepared for Change:** Life can throw curveballs. Perhaps you planned to study marine biology, but a summer internship at a tech company changes your mind. Being open to changing your path based on new experiences is a core aspect of Planned Happenstance.

The job market is constantly changing; many of the jobs that will exist in the future don't even exist yet. By adopting the principles of Planned Happenstance, you're preparing yourself to thrive in a world where flexibility and adaptability are essential. This approach helps reduce the pressure of having to figure out everything right now and encourages you to enjoy the journey of discovering your career. It also teaches us that while it's good to have goals and plans, it's equally important to **stay open to new experiences and be ready to adapt.** By embracing curiosity, persistence, flexibility, optimism, and a willingness to take risks, you can turn unexpected events into opportunities.

It's okay not to have all the answers. Stay open, stay curious, and be ready for the exciting possibilities that life might bring your way.

Fulfilling a career is not just about success—it's about satisfaction. It's about waking up every morning excited about what the day holds. It's about going to bed each night feeling accomplished and content.

This sense of fulfillment comes from making deliberate, informed decisions—decisions that honor who you are and what you aspire to be.

In the upcoming Chapter 5, we'll be focusing on resources and tools that will assist you throughout your career planning journey. From mentorship to online platforms and professional development opportunities, I'll guide you through using these resources to help you achieve your career objectives.

Exercise

Pros and Cons Evaluation Chart Worksheet

A pros and cons evaluation is a decision-making tool that helps you list the benefits and drawbacks of each potential career path you are considering. This visual chart allows you to weigh various factors and determine which career options are best suited to you.

You are at a critical stage where you're making important decisions about your future. Using a pros and cons chart, you can clearly see the positive and negative aspects of your career choice, which can help you make an informed and thoughtful decision.

How to Use It

- Write the career option you are considering at the top of the chart.
- Under the pros column, write the positive aspects of each career, such as job satisfaction, salary, growth opportunities, and alignment with your interests and skills.
- Under the cons column, write the negative aspects, including potential stressors, education or training required, job outlook, and any other personal concerns.
- Review your chart and consider which factors are most important to you. This will help you to compare and reflect on your options and guide your decision-making process.

Tips for Successful Research

- Prioritize quality over quantity. Pick the top factors that truly matter rather than listing every possible pro and con.
- Consider the long-term implications of each pro and con, not just immediate effects.
- Review your chart with someone you trust—a parent, teacher, or mentor—to get their perspective and advice.

Pros and Cons Evaluation Chart

Career Option: ______________________

Pros	**Cons**
• • • •	• • • •

Example:

Career Option: Graphic Designer

Pros	**Cons**
• Creative expression • Potential for remote work • Growing industry	• Competitive field • May require continual skill updates • Inconsistent freelance work

Which careers have more pros than cons?

Are there any cons that are deal-breakers for you?

Which pros fit best with your long-term goals and values?

How might any cons be mitigated or are they outweighed by the pros?

After completing the chart, spend some time reflecting on what you've written. Consider how you feel about the pros and cons you've listed. Are any patterns emerging that might guide your decision?

This worksheet is simply a tool to help you think through your career options. It's okay if you don't come to a firm conclusion immediately. Use it as a starting point and revisit it as you continue your career exploration and research.

Additional Notes

Chapter 5
Resources and Tools

When you believe in your dream and your vision, then it begins to attract its own resources. No one was born to be a failure.

Myles Munroe

From online career exploration platforms to personality tests, from industry reports to mentorship programs, each resource offers unique insights that can help shape your career decisions. But remember, these resources are not magic wands that will instantly reveal the perfect career path. Instead, they are aids that complement your self-exploration and decision-making processes.

By using these tools and resources well, you'll get a better idea of jobs that match up with what you like, what you're good at, and what you believe in. You'll also learn practical things like what kind of education you might need, how much you could earn, and where the job opportunities are growing—all of which help you make smarter choices about your future.

Curriculum Vitae vs Resume

A Curriculum Vitae, or CV for short, is your academic and professional biography rolled into one comprehensive document. The terms "CV" (Curriculum Vitae) and "resume" are often used interchangeably, but they do have some differences.

CV (Curriculum Vitae)

- A CV is typically longer than a resume and provides a comprehensive overview of a person's academic and professional background.
- It includes detailed information about education, employment, research, publications, presentations, awards, and other academic achievements.

Resume

- A resume is a shorter document that summarizes a person's relevant work experience, skills, education, and accomplishments.
- It's tailored to specific job applications and is usually limited to one or two pages and focuses more on work experience, skills, and achievements relevant to the position being applied for.

(I will call both documents CV in this book for easy reference.)

But what if your experience column reads like a brand-new notebook—pretty empty? Fear not! Everyone starts somewhere.

Here's how to bulk up a slim CV:

- **Highlight Academic Achievements:** Rocked a high GPA or scored big with an advanced project? Pop that on your CV. Employers love smarty-pants streaks.

- **Spotlight Classwork and Skills:** List relevant courses and detail the skills they've taught you. Did you learn to code in computer class or public speaking in English? That's gold for a CV.

- **Extracurricular Activities Shine:** Anything from debate club to sports can demonstrate team spirit, dedication, and leadership. If you've led a team or organized events, it's worth mentioning.

- **Volunteering Counts:** Helping out in community service shows you're proactive and possess a solid work ethic.

- **Certifications and Workshops:** Any extra learning you've lapped up can beef up your CV. Whether it's a first-aid certification or a digital marketing workshop, it shows you're no couch potato.

Tailor your CV and your cover letter to suit the role or program you're eyeing. And remember, what you lack in experience, you can often make up for with enthusiasm, fresh ideas, and a willingness to learn. Your CV isn't just a list of what you've done; it's a sneak preview of what you're capable of.

Check out Appendix 4 for more info about CVs.

LinkedIn Profile

Think of LinkedIn as a social media platform, but instead of sharing funny videos or pictures of your pets, it's all about your professional life.

Here's more information about this platform:

- **Professional Profile:** On LinkedIn, you create a profile that's like your online resume. You fill it with info about your education, any jobs you've had, and skills you've learned.

- **Connecting with People:** Just as on other social media, you can connect with friends, teachers, and people you've met. You can build a network of professional contacts.

- **Finding Jobs:** LinkedIn is a big place for job stuff. You can search for jobs, see what's out there, and even apply for some through the site.

- **Learning Sources:** There are also cool articles, videos, and courses on LinkedIn to help you learn new things and get better at stuff you already know.

Overall, it's a place where you can show off your professional side, connect with people in your field, and maybe even find your dream job one day.

Always check the Terms and Conditions when you register on web pages. The minimum age to sign up for LinkedIn is 16 years old in most countries.

Online Career Assessment Tools

These are digital resources designed to help you gain insights into your unique traits—your interests, personality, values, and skills. By understanding these aspects of yourself, it can help you establish the kind of career best suited to you.

There's a myriad of online tools available, each serving a different purpose.

- **Interest inventories,** for example, help you identify what you enjoy doing. These tests present various activities and ask how much you would like or dislike doing them. By answering honestly, you can discover careers that involve activities you enjoy.

- We already discussed **personality tests** in the previous chapters. Ever wondered why certain environments energize you while others drain you? The answer lies in your personality type. Understanding your personality type can help you identify careers where you're likely to thrive.

- **Value assessments** help show what matters most to you in life and work—things like caring for others, achieving status, or maintaining work-life balance. By knowing your core values, you can explore careers that satisfy these needs.

- **Skills assessments** are tools that evaluate your natural talents and learned abilities—things like critical thinking, communication skills, or artistic talents. By understanding your strengths, you can pursue careers where those skills are valued and utilized.

So how do you use these tools?

- Start by finding **a quiet place** free from distractions.

- As you go through the questions, **be honest** with yourself—there are no right or wrong answers here. The goal is to gain insights into yourself, not to fit into a preconceived notion of the 'ideal' career candidate.

- Once done, take time to **review the results.** What did they reveal about your interests, personality type, values, or skills? Are these insights the same as your current understanding of yourself? If there are surprises, that's okay—these tools are meant to spark self-reflection and exploration.

Always remember to review the Privacy Policy of any website before you begin, particularly if it asks for personal information. It's also good practice to look for reviews or validate the website's credibility to ensure it's a reputable source. While these online assessments can be informative and enjoyable, they should not replace professional advice for significant personal or career decisions.

These tools are just a part of your career journey. They provide insights but don't dictate your path. The final decision on which career to pursue lies in your hands, based on a combination of self-knowledge, research, and informed decision-making.

Career Counselors and Mentors

While online tools and resources are essential, they're just one piece of the career exploration puzzle. Another crucial component? People. More specifically, career counselors and mentors. These individuals can offer personalized guidance, share their experiences, and provide a unique perspective on your career journey.

- **Career counselors** are fantastic guides in the world of work. They are trained professionals who can help you understand your skills and interests, explore potential careers, and set achievable goals. They can also challenge pre-existing views or stereotypes around different job sectors and roles. Whether it's providing resources, helping you prepare for job interviews, or simply offering a listening ear during moments of uncertainty, career counselors can be invaluable allies in your career planning journey.

- Now let's look at **mentors.** These are individuals who have walked the path you're exploring and can share their insights and experiences. A mentor could be a teacher who inspires you, a family friend in a profession you admire, or even an industry professional you connect with on LinkedIn. The key is to find someone who is willing to share their knowledge and experiences with you.

So how do you secure a mentor?

- Start by identifying what you hope to **gain from the relationship.** Are you looking for guidance on choosing a college major?

Or perhaps advice on breaking into a specific industry? Once you have clarity on your needs, you can begin searching for individuals who can help meet them.

- When approaching potential mentors, **be respectful of their time** and express your appreciation for their expertise. Prepare for your initial meeting by doing your homework—research their background, understand their industry, and come prepared with thoughtful questions.

- Once you've established a mentoring relationship, **maintain open communication.** Be proactive in scheduling meetings or check-ins and come prepared to each session with specific questions or topics you'd like to discuss.

When meeting with a career counselor or mentor, remember that this is your journey—they are there to guide and support you, not to make decisions for you. **Ask insightful questions** that can help you make informed decisions about your future. Don't be afraid to **request feedback** on your plans or ideas—constructive criticism can provide valuable insights for your career planning.

Consider Emily, a high school junior interested in a career in environmental science. She sought guidance from her school's career counselor who helped her identify relevant college programs and potential career paths. But Emily didn't stop there. She reached out to a local environmental scientist she admired and asked if she could shadow her at work and seek her advice on her future career. The scientist agreed, and over the next few months, Emily gained invaluable firsthand experience and insights into the field she was passionate about. Her story illustrates the power of seeking guidance from career professionals. By leveraging the expertise of her career counselor, she was able to make informed decisions about her education and future career path.

No one expects you to navigate your career journey alone—there are people ready and willing to help guide your way.

Websites and Databases

We've explored the world of online assessments and the wisdom of career professionals, but what about other valuable resources on your career exploration journey? Career planning websites and databases.

These websites and databases are **goldmines of information,** packed with details about different industries, jobs, and what you need to get into them. You can find out everything from what a job involves to what kind of education you might need, how much you could make, and even how likely it is to grow in the future.

However, navigating these vast resources can feel overwhelming. Picture yourself in a library with thousands of books but no catalog or index to guide you. That's what exploring these websites can feel like without effective navigation strategies.

So how do you sift through this sea of information? Start by having a clear purpose.

Are you researching a specific profession or perhaps you're exploring an industry? Maybe you're curious about the educational requirements for a certain job role?

Whatever your purpose, having clarity can help you focus your research and find relevant insights amidst the information overload.

Once you have a purpose, use search features effectively. Most websites have **search bars** where you can type in keywords related to your research.

Some also offer **filters** that allow you to narrow down results based on criteria such as education level, industry, or location.

While exploring these sites, don't forget to **cross-reference information.** Just like in any research process, checking multiple sources enhances the reliability of your findings.

Here are some top picks for career planning websites and databases.

- First up is O*NET Online (onetonline.org). This is a comprehensive database offering detailed descriptions of various occupations by the U.S. Department of Labor. The site includes information on skills required, tasks involved, salary statistics, and more.

- Next is the Bureau of Labor Statistics (bls.gov, operated by the U.S. Department of Labor). This site provides in-depth information on various professions, including growth projections—a crucial factor to consider in career planning.

- Lastly, explore industry-specific websites. These offer detailed insights into specific fields—ideal if you have a clear industry preference.

If you are outside of the U.S.,
try to search the following keywords in your country:
occupation database / job description / salary statistics, etc.

Remember, these resources are tools designed to aid your exploration process—they don't dictate your path but illuminate potential ones. Your role is to use these insights, coupled with self-knowledge and guidance from professionals, to make informed decisions about your future career.

The power of these tools lies in their ability to complement your self-discovery and decision-making process. Always stay open-minded when you use these tools.

They can show you lots of options, but don't feel like you have to stick to what they say. Your career journey is all about you, and no tool can capture everything that makes you special. So, explore, learn, but always stay true to what feels right for you.

As we move into Chapter 6, we shift the focus to the application of everything you've learned. You'll gain insights into leaving lasting impressions, acing interviews, and effectively marketing your skills and values in whatever professional path you choose to tread.

Exercise

Mentor Interview Worksheet

A mentor interview is an opportunity for you to speak with someone who has experience and knowledge in a career field you're interested in. The goal is to learn from their journey, gain advice, and understand more about the industry and what it might be like to work in that field.

Connecting with a mentor can provide you with insights that aren't found in books or on websites. It's a chance for real-world learning and can help you make informed decisions about educational paths and career goals.

How to Use It

- Identify a mentor in a career field that interests you. This could be a professional you admire, a teacher, a family friend, or even someone you've learned about through your network who has agreed to help you.
- Contact and schedule a time to interview your mentor. This can be in person, over the phone, via e-mail, or through a video call.
- Plan your questions in advance using the space provided below. Consider what you really want to know about the career and what advice the mentor might have for someone just starting out.
- Conduct the interview respectfully and take notes in the space provided. Thank your mentor for their time and the information they've shared.

Tips for Successful Interview

- Be punctual.
- Dress appropriately if meeting in person or video calling.
- Listen actively and don't be afraid to ask follow-up questions.
- Be prepared to share a little about yourself and your ambitions.
- Finish by thanking them for their time and consider sending a follow-up thank you note after the interview.

Before the Interview

Prepare by researching your mentor's background and the field they work in. This will help you ask informed questions.

Mentor's Name: ______________________________

Date of Interview: ______________________________

Mentor's Background (Briefly describe your mentor's job title, industry, and years of experience.):

Your Career Interest Area:

Sample Questions for the Interview

Write your mentor's answers under the questions

What led you to this career path?

Can you describe a typical day in your job?

What do you enjoy most about your work?

What are some challenges you face in this field?

How do you see this industry changing in the next few years?

What skills or qualities do you think are important for success in this area?

How did you get your start in this field?

Can you recommend any resources (books, courses, websites) to learn more?

What advice would you give to someone interested in this field?

Your Questions for the Interview

Write your questions on the lines and your mentor's answers under the questions

Reflection Section

After completing the interview, reflect on what you learned and how it affects your understanding of the career field.

New Insights:

Confirmed Interests:

Areas for Further Exploration:

Changed Perceptions:

Next Steps for Your Career Planning:

Remember, the purpose of the interview is not to secure a job offer but to gain knowledge and advice. It's a learning experience that will help you in making informed decisions for your future career path. Use this worksheet as a guide to structure your interview and reflect on the knowledge gained.

Additional Notes

Chapter 6
Career Action Plan

It takes as much energy to wish as it does to plan.

Eleanor Roosevelt

You've journeyed far, exploring the terrain of your inner self and the landscape of career possibilities. Now, it's time to translate these insights into action. Welcome to the phase of creating a career action plan.

Think of a career action plan as a detailed roadmap for your career journey. It's not enough to know your destination—you need to chart out the route you'll take to get there.

A career action plan breaks down your long-term career goals into actionable steps. Instead of viewing your goal as one huge road trip, break it down into manageable sections. Each step you take brings you closer to your ultimate goal. But what makes a career action plan truly beneficial is its adaptability. Just like any journey, your career path may present unexpected detours or roadblocks. Your action plan isn't set in stone—it's a flexible guide that can adapt to these changes. It helps you identify potential obstacles and devise strategies to overcome them.

Now, let's roll up our sleeves and begin the process of creating your career action plan. Buckle up—it's time to turn those career dreams into an actionable reality.

Actionable Steps

You might have heard the saying "A journey of a thousand miles begins with a single step." Well, consider your long-term career goals as that thousand-mile journey. They represent your ultimate career aspirations—the job you dream of and the professional accomplishments you strive for. Setting these goals is vital because they give you direction, purpose, and a sense of what you're working toward.

But looking at that thousand-mile journey can feel daunting. That's where **breaking down long-term goals into actionable steps** comes in. This process transforms your career aspirations from abstract ideas into concrete tasks.

Imagine your long-term goal is to become a software engineer. Instead of viewing it as one enormous task, break it down.

- Enroll in a coding bootcamp or take online computer science courses.
- Focus on securing an internship at a tech company to gain hands-on experience.
- Aim for an entry-level job in the field to start building your career.

Each of these steps brings you closer to your ultimate goal.

Picture your long-term goal at the top of a ladder. Each rung below represents a smaller task leading up to that goal. Start at the bottom and work your way up, defining each step you need to take to reach the top.

But how do you determine these steps? That's where research comes in. Find out what it takes to achieve your goal—required skills, education, experience—and **turn those into tasks.**

Now grab a pen and paper—it's time for a worksheet activity.

Write down your long-term career goal at the top of the page. Then draw lines branching out from this goal, each line representing a smaller task leading up to it. Break these tasks down further into monthly, weekly, and even daily objectives.

For example, if one task is "Learn Python programming," your monthly objective could be "Complete an online Python course," your weekly objective might be "Master one module per week," and your daily objective could be "Spend one hour studying Python."

You can also use the previously learned **SMART method.** SMART criteria are guidelines used in setting objectives, making them more manageable and realistic. Ask yourself:

- Are they **Specific?**
  Do they clearly define what you want to achieve?

- Are they **Measurable?**
  Can you track your progress and know when you've achieved them?

- Are they **Achievable?**
  Can you realistically accomplish them given your resources and constraints?

- Are they **Relevant?**
  Do they align with your broader career aspirations?

- Are they **Time-Bound?**
  Do you have a clear time frame for achieving them?

Finally, let's talk about **visualization strategies**—tools that can help bring clarity to this planning process. Vision boards and goal maps provide a visual representation of your action plan.

Create a vision board by pasting pictures and phrases that represent your goals and the steps needed to achieve them onto a poster board.
Alternatively, draw a goal map with your career goal at the center and lines branching out toward smaller goals.

Using these visualization strategies can make your career journey feel more tangible and achievable. You're not just writing down tasks—you're creating a visual map leading to your dream.

Every journey starts with that first step—and every long-term career goal starts with actionable steps. So, start breaking down those goals.

Potential Obstacles

On your career journey, you're bound to encounter roadblocks. You might face obstacles related to your chosen career path, personal circumstances, or unforeseen events. However, remember that every successful individual you admire has navigated their own set of challenges. The key lies in resilience—the ability to bounce back from adversity and keep moving forward.

Anticipating potential challenges is a crucial step in your career planning process. Just as a chess player anticipates their opponent's moves, you need to predict the hurdles you might face in your chosen career path.

Perhaps your dream job requires an advanced degree, but tuition costs seem daunting. Maybe the industry you're interested in is highly competitive, with limited job openings. Or it could be a personal circumstance—a relocation for a family member's job or an unexpected health issue—that poses a challenge.

How can you anticipate these challenges?

Start by conducting thorough research on your chosen career path.

What are the common obstacles people face in this field?

Speak to professionals already working in the area and seek their advice. They've navigated this path before and can provide valuable insights.

Your personal circumstances also play a role in anticipating challenges. Reflect on your situation—financial constraints, family responsibilities—and consider how these factors might impact your career journey.

I have dedicated Chapter 7 to the challenges and obstacles you can encounter on this journey. After reading about the different kinds of roadblocks, you will learn how to develop resilience and perseverance.

Tracking Progress and Adapting the Plan

Tracking your progress is an essential step in your career action plan. Monitoring your progress ensures that you're on track.

- One of the most straightforward ways to track progress is by maintaining **a career journal.** This can be a physical notebook or a digital document where you record your accomplishments, challenges, and reflections related to your career journey. For instance, you could jot down any new skills you've learned, milestones you've reached, or obstacles you've overcome. Regularly updating this journal can provide a visual representation of your journey, helping you see how far you've come and what steps lie ahead.

- **Apps and digital tools** offer another method for tracking progress. Online platforms like Trello or Asana allow you to create task boards for your career goals. You can set deadlines, add notes, and mark tasks as completed as you progress. Seeing these completed tasks can give a sense of accomplishment, motivating you to continue working toward your goals.

- **Spreadsheets** are also effective for tracking progress, especially for quantifiable goals. For example, if one of your goals is to apply to ten internships over the summer, you could create a spreadsheet listing each application's status—submitted, awaiting response, interview scheduled, and so on.

Now let's discuss **flexibility** and **adaptation.** Think about a river—how it changes course depending on what's in its way. Well, your career plan should be like that too. It's okay to switch things up based on what's happening in your life and what you're learning. Maybe you will find out something new that makes you see a job in a different light. Or perhaps after trying out an internship, you realize it's not for you. It could even be that someone gives you advice that makes you think about a whole new career path you hadn't considered before. Being flexible means being open to these changes and adjusting your plan accordingly.

In these situations, it's essential to revisit your action plan and make necessary adjustments.

Your career action plan is not a static document—it evolves with you.

The **review and adjust** process involves regularly assessing your progress and adjusting your plan based on real-world feedback. Set aside time—maybe once a month or once a quarter—to review your action plan. Reflect on what's working well and what areas might need adjustment. Celebrate your progress, no matter how small, and use any setbacks as learning opportunities.

Your career journey is not a straight line—it's a winding path filled with twists and turns. By tracking your progress, staying flexible, and adapting your plan as needed, you'll be better equipped to navigate this journey and reach your career destination.

Your action plan isn't rigid—it's adaptable. It changes as you grow, as new information emerges, as circumstances shift. It's more than a static list—it's a living document that evolves with you.

So, keep this plan close. Let it be your guide as you navigate the world of career planning. Allow it to evolve with you, reflecting your growth and experiences.

In Chapter 7 we'll tackle challenges and obstacles you could encounter during your career journey. We will discuss strategies to face them head-on and turn difficulties into opportunities for growth and learning.

Exercise

Eisenhower Matrix Worksheet

This worksheet introduces you to the Eisenhower Matrix, a time management tool that helps you prioritize tasks based on their urgency and importance.

By using this method, you'll learn how to distinguish between tasks that demand immediate attention and those that can be scheduled for later or delegated.

The Eisenhower Matrix, also known as the Urgent-Important Matrix, is named after Dwight D. Eisenhower, the 34th President of the United States. He created this system to organize his tasks as a way to be more effective in both his military and presidential roles.

Imagine you've got a bunch of tasks to do for school or to plan your future. The Eisenhower Matrix is like a cool way to sort through them and figure out what's most important.

The matrix is a simple 2x2 grid that divides tasks into four categories:

- **Urgent and Important:** These are the things you have to do right away because they're super important. Like, if you have a big project due tomorrow or an important deadline to meet, those go here.

- **Important but Not Urgent:** These are things that are really important for your future, but you don't have to do them right this second. This could be stuff like researching careers you're interested in, studying for a test next week, or working on your college applications.

- **Urgent but Not Important:** These are things that seem really pressing, but they're not actually that important for your long-term goals. It could be stuff like checking your social media notifications or responding to texts from friends. They can wait while you focus on the important stuff.

- **Not Urgent and Not Important:** These are things that aren't super important and don't need to be done right away. They're the least urgent tasks, maybe things like watching TV or playing video games.

Don't forget, it's about working smarter, not harder. This worksheet is to help you focus on what really matters and steer clear of timewasters.

How to Use It

- **List** all the tasks you need to get done.
- **Assess** each task based on whether it's urgent (needs immediate action) or important (has significant consequences or benefits).
- **Place** each task in the corresponding quadrant on the matrix.
- **Take action** on the tasks based on their quadrant.

The Eisenhower Matrix

	Urgent	Not Urgent
Important	**INEVITABLE** Tasks with clear deadlines and consequences for not completing. **DO NOW**	**FUTURE PLANNING** Tasks or long-term goals that require strategic thinking, no set deadline. **SCHEDULE**
Not Important	**BUSY WORK** Tasks that need to be done but don't require your specific skill set. **DELEGATE**	**TIME WASTERS** Tasks that distract you from your goals and add no measurable value. **DELETE**

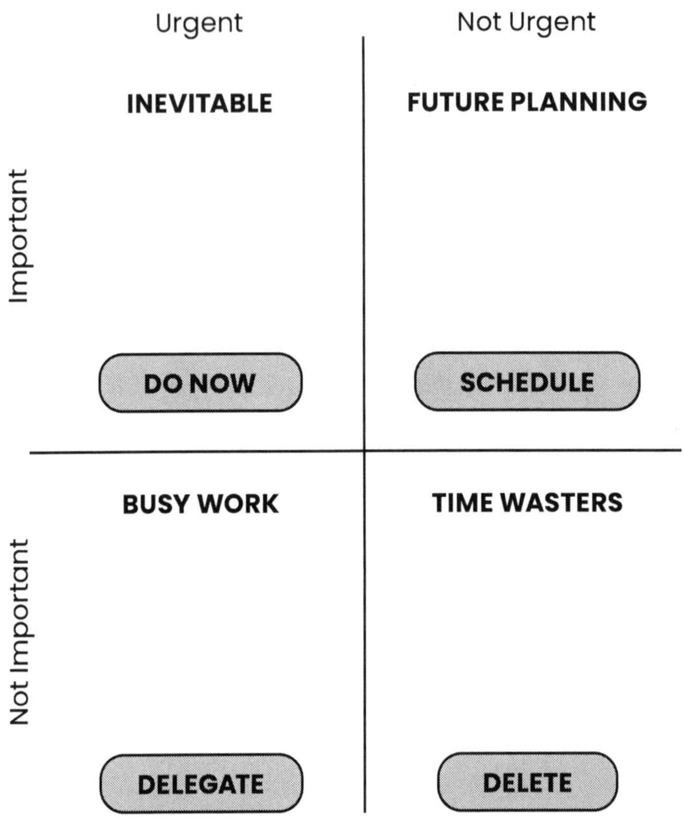

Reflection Section

Are you often mistaking urgent tasks for important ones?

How can you delegate tasks more effectively?

What sort of tasks can you eliminate to free up more time for important things?

Additional Notes

Chapter 7
Challenges and Obstacles

Everything negative—pressure, challenges—is all an opportunity for me to rise.

Kobe Bryant

Time to get real—life throws us curveballs, especially when it comes to figuring out our careers. You might feel unsure about what you want to do, or maybe your friends or family are putting pressure on you. And let's not forget about the stress of making big decisions that could shape your future. It's all part of the ride, but you're not alone in facing these challenges.

You may find yourself questioning your abilities, comparing yourself to others, or grappling with fear of the unknown. It's natural to feel overwhelmed. But remember this:

Challenges are not roadblocks; they are opportunities for growth.

This chapter is dedicated to helping you navigate these complexities. It builds upon the core competencies you've developed in earlier chapters, equipping you with strategies and techniques to face and overcome these obstacles.

But what happens when you hit a bump in the road?
How do you maintain momentum to keep striving for your goals when faced with obstacles?

This is where **resilience** comes into play. Resilience is the ability to bounce back from adversity and continue moving forward despite challenges. It's about being flexible in your thinking, adapting to changes, and maintaining a positive outlook.

The good news is that resilience can be developed and strengthened, much like a muscle.

As you overcome obstacles by finding your way around them, you will grow.

There are several common challenges you might encounter in your career planning process—let's explore these and how to overcome them.

Lack of Motivation

I'd like to talk about something everyone faces at some point—lack of motivation. You're thinking about career choices, but it seems as huge as Everest, doesn't it? And it feels like the easiest thing is to just say, "Nah, I can deal with this tomorrow... or maybe the day after," and shove it off, right? That's perfectly okay. We all feel like that sometimes.

Think about it this way: career planning isn't about scaling a mountain in one huge leap. It's more like tackling a video game. You play each level separately, right? You defeat the enemies, learn the tricks and traps, gain experience, and then move on to the next level. There's no rush! So, why not approach career planning the same way?

Are you into music? How about dedicating an afternoon to discovering all the exciting roles in the music industry?

Do you feel a thrill when you're coding? Use a few free hours to explore the tech world—from startups to big corporations, there's a ton to discover!

You're not signing a lifelong contract here. You're just browsing, gathering information, seeing what piques your interest.

Too often, we can put a huge amount of pressure on ourselves to have our whole life figured out. But guess what? You don't have to. **It's okay not to know everything right away.** It's okay to explore, to take your time. This is your future and it should unfold at your pace.

Breaking down the enormity of career planning into smaller, more digestible pieces can make things less overwhelming. And, who knows, you might just surprise yourself on how far you can go when you take it one level at a time.

Uncertainty and Indecision

Uncertainty and indecision can feel like a dense fog, obscuring your vision and making the path ahead seem uncertain. It's a common feeling when you're at the beginning of your career planning journey, standing at the crossroads of multiple potential paths. But here's a little secret:

It's okay to feel uncertain. In fact, it's perfectly normal.

Consider the story of Ariana, a bright high school senior with interests in both art and science. She felt torn between pursuing a career in medical research or becoming a professional illustrator. Her fear of making the wrong choice led to indecision and stress.

What did Ariana do?

She started by acknowledging her uncertainty instead of running away from it. She understood that this was a significant decision, and it was okay to take time to explore her options.

Ariana methodically evaluated her choices using simple yet effective tools like pros and cons lists and different scenarios. She listed down potential outcomes for each career path, imagining what her life might look like in each scenario. This didn't dispel her uncertainty completely but gave her a clearer picture of what each path entailed.

She also used the **Eisenhower Matrix** (the exercise from the previous chapter), a decision-making tool that helps prioritize tasks based on their urgency and importance. Ariana identified which aspects of her decision were most critical and needed immediate attention.

But she didn't stop there. Ariana took advantage of resources available to her—she sought guidance from **mentors, teachers, and professionals** in both fields. She also utilized career assessments that helped clarify her interests and match them with potential career paths.

After several weeks of careful contemplation, research, and mentor-guided exploration, Ariana stumbled upon a field that she'd never considered before—medical illustration. It was a perfect merger of her two passions. Medical illustrators use their design and art skills to create illustrations, diagrams, and animations for medical and scientific purposes. Their work helps explain complex medical concepts in ways that can be understood by doctors, students, and sometimes even patients. The more she discovered, the more Ariana realized this was a field that perfectly synergized her love for art and her fascination with medicine and science. Medical illustration allowed her to bring complex scientific concepts to life through art, acting as the visual bridge between medicine and patient education.

Ariana's story is an inspiration for anyone facing a crossroads, torn between passions. It demonstrates that sometimes a bit of courage and lots of exploration can lead you to something unexpected and ideal.

Through her story you can see that with enough determination and creativity, you can carve out a unique path for yourself, even if that means combining two different fields into a career that is as unique as you are.

External Pressures and Expectations

Now, let's turn our attention to a different kind of challenge: external pressures and expectations. These are the **expectations that come from family, friends, and society** at large about what you "should" do with your career. It's not uncommon to feel the weight of these expectations on your shoulders.

Sometimes, your parents might want you to do the same job as them or go for a really fancy career. Your friends might think certain jobs are super awesome or make a lot of money. And society in general tends to think that some jobs are better than others; remember the part about non-traditional career paths?

These outside influences can make it tough to pick a career that's right for you. They might push you to do something that's not really your thing, even if it doesn't match up with what you like, what you're good at, or what you care about. It's important to think about what you really want, not what other people think you should do.

So, how can you manage these pressures without compromising your own career aspirations?

Here are some strategies:

- **Assertive Communication:** Assertiveness is the ability to express your thoughts and feelings in a respectful yet firm manner. It involves standing up for your rights without violating the rights of others. In the context of career planning, assertive communication allows you to articulate your career goals and aspirations to others while acknowledging their opinions and concerns.

  For example, if your parents want you to pursue a career in medicine but your passion lies in graphic design, an assertive response might be: "I understand why you think medicine is a good choice for me, but I truly enjoy graphic design and believe I can build a successful career in it."

- **Negotiation Techniques:** Sometimes, managing external pressures involves finding a middle ground. This is where negotiation techniques come into play. To negotiate well, it's all about seeing things from the other person's point of view and finding a solution that works for both of you.

  For instance, if your parents are worried about the financial stability of a career in art, perhaps you could propose a double major in art and business or discuss different roles within the art industry that offer financial stability.

- **Role Play Scenarios:** Practicing these conversations beforehand can be extremely helpful. Consider role-playing with a friend or mentor. Script out what you want to say and anticipate possible responses. This can help you feel more prepared and confident when having these conversations in real life.

- **Balance and Boundary-Setting:** While it's important to listen to advice from others, it's equally crucial to set boundaries. This involves clearly communicating your needs and decisions while respecting the thoughts and feelings of others.

You don't have to please everyone—it's important to find a balance between external expectations and your own career aspirations.

Resilience and Perseverance

You've faced uncertainty and navigated external pressures, but how do you build up the all-important resilience? Resilience is the capacity to recover quickly from difficulties, to bounce back from setbacks, and keep going in the face of adversity.

Why is resilience so important in career planning?

It's simple. The path to your ideal career won't always be smooth. Resilience equips you with the mental and emotional toughness needed to face challenges head-on and bounce back stronger.

Here are some strategies for developing resilience:

- Set **achievable milestones** (as we already learned in Chapter 6—Career Action Plan). Breaking down your long-term goals into smaller, achievable tasks can help maintain motivation and prevent feelings of overwhelm. Achieving these milestones gives you a sense of progress and success, which can fuel your resilience.

- Engage in **reflective practices.** Reflection allows you to learn from your experiences—both successes and failures. When faced with a setback, instead of viewing it as a failure, see it as a learning opportunity. What can you do differently next time? What did this experience teach you?

Consider the story of Perla, a young aspiring chef who was initially rejected by several culinary schools. Instead of giving up on her dream, Perla reflected on her experiences.

She realized that she needed more hands-on experience to strengthen her application. So, she took a job at a local restaurant and honed her culinary skills. A year later, she reapplied and was accepted into one of her top-choice schools.

- Don't underestimate the power of **mentorship.** A mentor or support group can provide guidance, encouragement, and constructive feedback—all crucial elements in building resilience. Share your challenges with them; their perspectives may shed new light on the situation or offer solutions you hadn't considered.

- Keep your **motivation** levels high. Techniques such as daily affirmations, maintaining a success journal, and visualizing can help keep your spirits up. Remind yourself regularly of why you chose this career path and what achieving your goal would mean to you.

Resilience involves facing challenges and difficulties with courage, learning from them, and emerging stronger. Welcome the challenges that come your way.

Developing Strategies

Now that we've learned how to be resilient, let's see how we can develop strategies for the previously mentioned challenges. Developing contingency plans involves proactive problem-solving and adaptability skills. It means having a Plan B, C, D, and E if Plan A doesn't work out.

There's **no one-size-fits-all solution** when it comes to overcoming obstacles. The strategies you develop should be tailored to your situation, career goals, and the specific challenges you anticipate.

Here are some tips to guide you:

- **Identify the Problem:** Start by clearly defining the obstacles in your path. What's holding you back? Is it tuition costs, lack of experience, or a competitive job market? Understanding the problem is the first step to solving it.

- **Find Solutions:** Once you've identified the challenges, brainstorm possible solutions. If tuition costs are an issue, explore scholarships, financial aid, or part-time work. If the job market in your chosen field is tough, consider related fields where your skills could be applied.

- **Adapt and Overcome:** Cultivate adaptability as a key strength. In today's ever-changing world, the ability to learn new skills, embrace new technologies, and adjust to changing circumstances will help you tackle obstacles and thrive in your career journey.

Here are some real-life examples of how individuals overcame career-related obstacles. These case studies serve as reminders that obstacles are not dead ends—they're merely detours on the path to success.

Take the story of Samantha, who dreamed of becoming a veterinarian but faced academic challenges in college. Despite her passion, her grades weren't high enough for veterinary school. Samantha shifted strategies, dedicating a year to strengthening her application. She volunteered at animal shelters, shadowed vets, and took additional courses to improve her science background. This persistence paid off; Samantha was eventually accepted into a veterinary program.

Tim, an aspiring journalist whose multiple internship applications were rejected, didn't give up. Instead, he started a local news blog covering community events. The blog gained traction, showcasing Tim's capabilities to potential employers.

Soon after, Tim landed a prestigious media internship, turning earlier rejections into a springboard for success.

These cases exemplify the power of resilience and adaptability. Whether redirecting energy to improve their position or creating their own opportunities, individuals like Samantha and Alex demonstrate that obstacles can be stepping stones to future victories.

You have the strategies to navigate uncertainty and overcome times when you may lack motivation. You also have learned how to manage external pressures and build resilience. Reflecting on your experiences gives you the chance to learn from them and alters your course of action, if needed. Now you have the courage to confront challenges head-on and transform them into a way to help you gain success.

Next up, in Chapter 8, we will discuss the importance of flexibility and how to adjust our career choices.

Exercise

Challenge Anticipation Worksheet

The purpose of this worksheet is to help you foresee potential challenges you might encounter as you progress through the steps to get you to your career goals. By acknowledging these challenges in advance, you can prepare strategies to overcome them, making you better equipped and more resilient on your career path.

How to Use It

- Reflect on your career goals and the path you plan to take to achieve them.
- Think about possible challenges or obstacles you may face along this path.
- Fill in the table on page 122, identifying these potential challenges and developing strategies for overcoming them.
- Keep this worksheet handy and refer back to it regularly as you progress in your career planning. It can serve as a reminder of your problem-solving approaches and help you navigate any difficulties you encounter.

Tips for Completion

- Be as specific as possible with both challenges and strategies; the more detailed your plan, the more prepared you'll be.
- Don't be afraid to list challenges that seem daunting; acknowledging them is the first step to overcoming them.
- Remember, some challenges may require multiple strategies; don't limit yourself to just one.
- Consult with mentors, peers, or educators if you're struggling to come up with strategies or identify resources.
- Use this worksheet in conjunction with your career action plan to create a comprehensive plan for your future.

Potential Challenge	**Example:** Difficulty being accepted into a preferred college program
Strategy to Overcome	**Example:** Apply to multiple programs, seek alternative certifications, gain related experience
Resources Needed	**Example:** College application materials, information on alternative programs, connection to a mentor in the field
Timeline for Action	**Example:** Complete applications by November, research alternatives by December, begin volunteering in January

Potential Challenge	
Strategy to Overcome	
Resources Needed	
Timeline for Action	

Reflection Section

After you've filled out the table, take some time to reflect on the strategies you've developed.

What did you learn about your approach to problem-solving?

Which potential challenges do you feel most prepared to handle now, and which do you need to further research or seek advice on?

How do you feel about your career path and goals after completing this exercise?

Keep this worksheet as a living document, updating strategies and challenges as you move forward and as circumstances change. Your adaptability will be a tremendous asset.

Additional Notes

Chapter 8
Adjusting Career Choices

It's our choices... that show what we truly are, far more than our abilities.

J. K. Rowling

Career planning is a continuous process and a natural part of personal and professional growth. It's not a straight line from Point A to Point B but a series of twists and turns, detours, and dead ends. And just as a sailor adjusts their course in response to changing winds and currents, you too must be prepared to evaluate and adjust your career path in response to changing circumstances.

You see, choosing a career path doesn't involve finding out about the perfect job that will make you happy forever, but it does involve finding the perfect job for now. It's important that you are open to the possibility that this might change over time.

Maybe you start doing something, but it doesn't make you as happy as you thought it would. Or you discover you're into something else now. Perhaps changes in your personal life require you to reconsider your career goals. And sometimes new jobs pop up because of new tech or changes in what companies need.

Whatever the case may be, it's important to **take time periodically to reflect** on your personal satisfaction and fulfillment in your chosen career path.

Are you still excited by what you do?
Does it still fit with your interests, skills, and values?
Is this the only path that will bring you satisfaction or fulfillment?

If the answer to any of these questions is no, then it's time to consider career transitions and alternative paths. It's time to explore new interests, acquire new skills, or reevaluate your values. It's time to seek continuous learning and professional development opportunities that can help you move to a new career path or advance in your current one.

This chapter is about embracing change and uncertainty and seeing them as opportunities for growth and exploration. It's about recognizing that your career path is not set in stone but can be reshaped and reimagined over time. And it's about empowering you with the tools and strategies you need to evaluate and adjust your career path as you continue on your journey.

Personal Satisfaction

You stand at a crossroads in your career journey, equipped with the knowledge of your interests, skills, and values, and guided by the compass of your long-term goals. But as you gaze down each potential path, you're confronted with an essential question:

Does this path lead to personal satisfaction and fulfillment?

Self-reflection serves as a vital tool in answering this question. It's like holding up a mirror, allowing you to see clearly where you've been, where you are now, and where you might be headed.

Begin by asking yourself:

How satisfied are you with your current career path?
Does it bring you joy and fulfillment?
Does it still align with your interests, skills, and values?
Do you really like your job,
or do you wish you were doing something else?
Are there other paths that might bring you more satisfaction
or fulfillment?

Consider keeping a **career journal** to document your thoughts and feelings about your work. Journal prompts such as "What aspect of my job brings me the most satisfaction?" or "What tasks do I find most draining?" can provide valuable insights into what aspects of your job fit well with your interests and values, and which ones don't.

Self-assessment quizzes can also be useful tools in gauging your satisfaction with your current career path. These quizzes can help identify areas of dissatisfaction and potential avenues for change.

Meet Lindsey, a successful lawyer who found herself increasingly dissatisfied with her high-pressure job. Through self-reflection exercises, she realized that, while she enjoyed advocating for her clients, she craved more creative expression in her work. She decided to transition into a career as a legal consultant for a television network, where she could combine her legal expertise with her passion for storytelling.

Like Lindsey, you might find that self-reflection leads you to reconsider your current career path. You might discover new interests or passions that pull you in a different direction. Or you might find that certain aspects of your job no longer sit right with your values.

This is where the concept of **career check-ups** comes into play. Just as you would visit a doctor for a physical check-up, you should periodically conduct a career check-up to assess your satisfaction and fulfillment in your chosen career. This involves systematically reviewing your career situation to ensure it still feels right in relation to your personal goals and values.

Whether it's every six months or once a year, schedule time to reflect on your career journey.

It's okay to change course if you're not satisfied with where you're headed. Your career journey is not set in stone but can be reshaped and reimagined over time. Welcome change and uncertainty as opportunities for growth and exploration. After all, the goal of your career journey is not just to find a job but to find personal satisfaction and fulfillment.

Career Transitions and Alternative Paths

There comes a point in your career journey when you might gaze at the path ahead and wonder, "Is this really where I want to go?" Perhaps the road you've been traveling on no longer brings you joy. Maybe you've discovered new interests that don't fit in with your current path. Or perhaps changes in your personal life have sparked a desire for something different.

This is where the notion of **career transitions** can help. A career transition is essentially a shift from one career path to another. It's standing at a fork in the road and choosing to take a different path—one that might be unfamiliar but holds the promise of new opportunities and experiences.

Career transitions can be daunting, they involve stepping out of your comfort zone and venturing into uncharted territory.

But they also offer an opportunity for growth and exploration, and it can be an exciting time too.

So, how do you navigate a career transition?

How do you explore alternative paths and determine which one might be right for you?

- One effective way is through **informational interviews.** These are informal conversations with professionals in the field you're interested in. They can provide valuable insights into what it's like to work in that field, what skills are required, and what opportunities are available. Unlike your first ever informational interviews when you were initially setting out, these ones can include more questions regarding where you are currently at in your career journey and how the skills and experiences you've achieved whilst on this path can then be useful in this new field of work too.

- Consider **reaching out to people** in your network who work in the field you're interested in. Invite them for a coffee and chat or a virtual meet-up. Prepare a list of questions to ask—similar to Appendix 1.

- **Volunteering** can also provide hands-on experience in a new field. This involves volunteering your time to gain practical experience. This should give you a feel for what it's like to work in that area and whether it feels right for you.

- **Transferable skills** are another crucial aspect of career transitions. These are skills you've acquired in your current career that can be applied to a new career. For example, if you've developed strong communication skills in your current job, these can be transferred to a variety of other fields. Take some time to identify your transferable skills.

What skills have you developed in your current job or training? How might these be applicable to the new field you're interested in?

- **Mapping out connections** between your experiences and potential new directions can also be helpful. This involves identifying the skills, knowledge, and experiences you've gained in your current career and how these might be applicable to a new career.

When going through a career transition, you aren't leaving behind your past, you're building upon it. You're using what makes you special—your skills, what you know, and what you've been through—to find a new way forward that fits what you're into now, what's important to you, and what's going on in your life.

Lifelong Learning

Finding a career that makes you happy means always learning new stuff and finding chances to get better at what you do. With lifelong learning you will keep up with the latest trends, add more qualifications to your CV, feed your curiosity, expand your horizons, and stay adaptable in an ever-evolving job market.

You might wonder, "Why should I invest time and energy into learning something new when I'm already swamped with my current job responsibilities?" But think of it this way, **professional development** isn't just about doing your current job better. It's about preparing yourself for future opportunities. It's about honing your skills, broadening your knowledge, and becoming more versatile and adaptable. Of course, if you are happy and fulfilled in your current pathway, then that's okay!

There's a world of learning opportunities out there waiting for you to explore if you feel ready for a change. You might choose to delve into **self-directed learning,** where you take charge of your own education.

This could involve reading industry publications, attending webinars, and/or listening to podcasts in your field.

Professional courses and certifications are another avenue for learning. These provide structured learning experiences and can enhance your credibility in your field. They can be a significant commitment of time and money, so it's essential to choose wisely based on your career goals and interests.

Mentorship can also be a powerful tool for professional development. A mentor can provide guidance, feedback, and advice based on their own experiences. They can challenge you to stretch beyond your comfort zone and support you as you cope with challenges along the way.

Here are some resources to jumpstart your continuous learning journey:

- **Coursera:** An online platform offering courses from top universities and companies worldwide.

- **Udemy:** A platform offering a wide range of online courses on various topics.

- **LinkedIn Learning:** Offers video courses taught by industry experts in software and business skills.

- **TED Talks:** These are short, powerful presentations given by experts, innovators, and thought leaders from around the world. The speakers share their insights, experiences, and expertise on a particular subject, aiming to inspire, inform, and provoke thoughts in the audience.

- **Industry Associations:** Many industry associations offer professional development resources, including webinars, workshops, conferences, and networking events.

The key to continuous learning is curiosity and an open mind. Don't be afraid to step out of your comfort zone and explore new topics. And remember that every learning experience, whether it's a success or a failure, is an opportunity for growth.

So go ahead, take the leap into the world of continuous learning. Your future self will thank you.

Continuous personal growth and learning are invaluable assets on your career journey. You will keep adding to your skills and knowledge, and become a more versatile, adaptable, and resilient individual.

Moving onto Chapter 9, I invite you to imagine "You in the World of Work." Stepping into the professional world is an exciting new frontier teeming with life-changing experiences and opportunities. Get ready to explore how you can navigate these waters proactively, tactfully, and successfully. Forward we go.

Exercise

Professional Development Plan Worksheet

A professional development plan is a strategic document that outlines your goals for professional growth and the steps you need to take to achieve them. This tool helps you focus on acquiring new skills, knowledge, and experiences necessary to advance in your chosen career or change to a new one.

How to Use It

- Reflect on your career goals and the skills or knowledge you need to reach these goals.
- Research and identify opportunities that could help you develop these skills or knowledge (e.g., online courses, internships, and mentorships).
- Fill out the sections on page 134 to create your professional development plan.
- Keep this plan accessible, review it often, and update it as your goals and interests evolve.

Tips for Completion

- Be ambitious but also realistic; setting goals that stretch your abilities without being out of reach will keep you motivated.
- Consider various types of opportunities such as online learning, volunteering, part-time jobs, or even hobby projects that could contribute to your skill set.
- Regularly scheduled progress checkpoints allow you to celebrate small successes and recalibrate if necessary.
- Remember that professional development is an ongoing process and not a onetime task. It requires dedication and persistence.

Development Goal	**Example:** Improve public speaking
Skills/Knowledge Needed	**Example:** Confidence, articulation, engagement strategies
Opportunities to Learn/Develop	**Example:** Join a local Toastmasters club, attend a public speaking workshop
Timeline	**Example:** Join by June, workshop in August
Progress Checkpoints	**Example:** Practice speech monthly, evaluate improvements biannually

Development Goal	
Skills/Knowledge Needed	
Opportunities to Learn/Develop	
Timeline	
Progress Checkpoints	

Reflection Section

What excites you most about your goals and the process of working toward them?

How do your professional development goals fit with your long-term career aspirations?

What steps can you take immediately to begin working on these goals?

Use this worksheet as a living document throughout your learning and career journey to guide you and keep track of your professional development.

Additional Notes

Chapter 9
You in the World of Work

The best preparation for tomorrow is doing your best today.

H. Jackson Brown, Jr.

As we explore this final chapter, it's important to remember that there is no one-size-fits-all approach when it comes to career journeys. Your path will be uniquely yours—shaped by your passions, guided by your purpose, and paved with your decisions. For some it may not be as winding, it may only have a few bumps or pauses. For others, it may be more of a winding road filled with detours, pit stops, and views to admire. Both are valid and both are worth celebrating.

Change is also an integral part of this journey. As you grow and evolve, so too may your career interests and goals. This is not something to fear but rather something to embrace. After all, the ability to adapt to change is a valuable skill in today's rapidly evolving job market.

Entering the working world after years of education is a significant step in your life. Many new experiences await you: your first project, your first work-related challenge, your first performance-review, and more. These experiences are all part of your professional journey.

Having a successful career involves lots of things, technical skills you've gained from school, experiences you gain along the way, and personal skills you will develop when navigating this exciting yet sometimes challenging path. These abilities are all part of becoming the best version of "You in the World of Work."

Office Dynamics

Every workplace has its unique blend of patterns, behaviors, and relationships. Understanding these dynamics can be essential in helping you excel in your career.

Imagine **office dynamics** as a dance. Every dancer has a role, and understanding each other's movement is crucial for keeping rhythm. Similarly, in the workplace, everyone from the CEO (Chief Executive Officer) to the intern plays a vital part. Recognizing the roles, behavior, and interactions of your colleagues can help you adapt, communicate effectively, and contribute positively.

Take, for example, Rose, who recently joined a tech firm as a project manager. Rose noticed her team was made up of independent, dedicated professionals who preferred clear guidance and then the freedom to execute their tasks. Instead of micro-managing, Rose provided explicit instructions and goals and then stepped back, allowing her team to work in the way they were most comfortable. The end result was an empowered, motivated team that delivered high-quality work.

Now consider Robert, an accountant at a small non-profit. Robert quickly realized that the organization's size made it more like a family, with open communication and everyone helping out beyond their specific roles. He embraced this culture, volunteering to assist with community outreach events despite it not being part of his job description. His involvement led to a better relationship with his colleagues and a broader understanding of the organization.

What patterns do you observe in successful office or group environments you know?
How can understanding these dynamics make you a better team member or leader?
How do these dynamics affect productivity and satisfaction?

In the upcoming week, observe the dynamics in your office or any group setting that you're a part of. Identify the roles, communication styles, and hierarchy, and think about how you can contribute positively to the group.

Understanding office dynamics involves observation and effective participation. The more adept you become at 'the office dance,' the more you'll enjoy your workplace and the greater your potential for success.

Workplace Challenges

Workplace challenges are an inevitable part of your career journey. Whether it's meeting **tight deadlines,** dealing with **difficult colleagues,** or working through **challenging projects,** the key lies not in avoiding these hurdles but in learning how to effectively navigate them.

Managing workload and combating creative burnouts are common struggles. For example, Jake, a software developer, found himself overwhelmed by his workload and was close to burnout. Instead of allowing this to hinder his performance, Jake communicated his difficulties to his manager. They discussed stress management and delegation strategies, enabling him to tackle his workload without sacrificing creativity or productivity.

It's important to remember that everyone experiences times of fatigue, and it's absolutely alright to ask for help and prioritize self-care.

Addressing issues with superiors or colleagues can be another challenging aspect. When Mike had a disagreement with his supervisor over a project, rather than letting it fester, he chose to address it professionally.

He requested a meeting, expressed his concerns diplomatically, and was open to feedback. As a result, they were able to align their expectations and work more harmoniously.

How would you handle a similar situation?
Can you identify strategies that would help mitigate these kinds of challenges?

Here's a list of strategies to help tackle common workplace problems:

- **Effective Communication:** Clear and concise communication can prevent misunderstandings while promoting a productive work environment.

- **Emotional Intelligence:** Understanding, managing, and effectively expressing your own emotions, as well as understanding others' emotions, can reduce conflicts and improve relationships at work.

- **Time Management:** Prioritizing tasks, avoiding procrastination, and maintaining work-life balance can combat stress and increase productivity.

- **Positive Attitude:** Maintaining positivity during stressful situations can foster a calm, problem-solving approach, helping find solutions easier.

- **Developing Resilience:** Embrace challenges as opportunities to learn and grow. Resilience can help in bouncing back from setbacks.

- **Seeking Feedback and Constructive Criticism:** Regular feedback helps to identify areas for improvements.

- **Building Relationships:** Fostering good relationships with colleagues can improve morale and communication, and assist with networking opportunities.

- **Conflict Resolution Skills:** Dealing with conflicts in a calm and efficient manner prevents escalation and helps maintain a healthy workplace environment.

- **Seeking Help When Needed:** Don't hesitate to ask for assistance or advice when needed. This is a sign of strength and a willingness to learn.

Overcoming these challenges often boils down to effective communication, maintaining professionalism, prioritizing self-care, and staying focused on your work.

Remember, challenges are opportunities for growth, and navigating them successfully can significantly boost your career progression.

Career Agility

In an ever-evolving world, industries transform, job roles adapt, and new professions emerge. This is where career agility comes in. Being agile in your career means having the ability to adapt to new situations and demands swiftly and efficiently. It's about staying relevant in a dynamic job market, being open to learning new skills, and having a willingness to shift directions when necessary.

"How do I cultivate **career agility**?" you may ask.

- The answer lies in **continued education and skill development.** No matter what field you're in, there's always room for growth and improvement. Continued education doesn't necessarily mean going back to school for another degree; it can be as simple as attending workshops, taking online courses, or even reading up on industry trends.

By constantly honing your skills and expanding your knowledge base, you maintain your relevance in your chosen field. Moreover, it increases your adaptability to transition into new roles or industries, should you choose to do so.

- Another strategy for managing career changes is cultivating a **flexible mindset.** Flexibility involves seeing the opportunities for growth that change can bring. It's about being comfortable with uncertainty and having the confidence to take on new challenges. Training yourself to think flexibly can be as simple as setting small daily challenges or changing your routine regularly.

- A personal **SWOT analysis** can also be a useful tool in managing career changes. By assessing your Strengths, Weaknesses, Opportunities, and Threats, you gain insight into your current career status and where you might want to go next. It allows you to identify areas where you excel and areas that need improvement.

A SWOT analysis is a tool that helps you figure out what you're good at and what you might need to work on. Check out Appendix 5 to get more information on this.

- **Expert advice** can be invaluable when considering a career transition. Career coaches or mentors who have navigated their own career changes can provide guidance and insights based on their experiences. They can help you identify signs indicating a need for change and offer strategies to approach it effectively.

Seeking Support

Seeking support when things get overwhelming at work can often be the difference between maintaining a healthy work-life balance and succumbing to stress or burnout. Understanding where and how to seek support is crucial in these situations.

- Having open conversations with your **team or supervisor** plays a pivotal role in managing work stress. Transparent communication about your stress can lead to productive solutions, like redistributing workload or exploring flexible working hours. Importantly, it can help establish a more supportive and understanding work environment.

- **Human Resources (HR)** plays a significant role in managing work-related stress. They can help devise solutions to workplace issues, mediate conflicts, or provide resources for managing stress.

- In times of excessive stress, it might be beneficial to consult a **medical doctor.** If you're experiencing signs of chronic stress—including constant fatigue, headaches, anxiety, or other physical symptoms—seeking medical advice is crucial.

If you're feeling overwhelmed at work, don't hesitate to reach out to the appropriate parties—whether that be your supervisor, HR, or your doctor. No one is expected to handle everything alone, especially when it threatens your well-being.

Seeking timely support when overwhelmed not only helps manage stress but fosters a healthier work environment. Your wellness is essential and prioritizing it helps you and your career in the long run.

Re-evaluating Your Career Choice

Examining your job choices is a big part of personal growth. It involves pausing to make sure your job matches your interests, what you value in life, and your future plans.

Signs that you're in the wrong job:

- You don't feel excited or motivated about your work.
- You feel tired or like your work doesn't mean anything.
- Your job doesn't use your skills and talents.
- You always wish you were doing something else.
- The values of your job don't match your personal values.

Before deciding to change your job, figure out if your current work issues can be fixed. Maybe a chat with your boss might bring some change, or learning some new things, or moving to a different project or team can help.

What parts of your job do you not like?
Can these things be fixed without
having to change your job completely?

If changing your job seems like the best idea, you should start by figuring out what you want from your next one. Look into different roles that you are interested in and match your abilities.

- Make a list of jobs that interest you.
- Meet and talk to people who work in these jobs.

- Compare the good and bad points of each job.
- Plan how to move to a new job, including learning new things, updating your resume, and getting ready for interviews.

Take a moment to think about how happy you are with your current job. If you find that you're not happy most of the time, start looking into other careers that might suit you better.

It's okay to stop and think about your career choices. You work a lot of your life, so it's important to have a job that makes you happy, has a purpose, and fulfills you as a person.

Exercise

Identifying Your Job/Activity Happiness Levels Worksheet

Let's find out how much you really enjoy your part-time job, school activities, or those after-school responsibilities! Figuring this out can help you understand what you like and what you don't. This way, you'll have a clearer picture of what to look for in a future job. Let's explore!

How to Use It

Give honest and detailed answers (no one is going to see this but you)—there's no right or wrong answer here. It's all about self-discovery!

Tips for Completion

- Try not to rush this. Take your time to think about your answers.
- Honesty is key. The more sincere you are, the more helpful the exercise will be.
- If you're stuck, think about a typical day and take it from there. What tasks bring a smile to your face? Which ones make you frown?
- Don't sweat over exact ratings, it's just a rough estimate of how things feel to you.

Part 1: Break Down Your Responsibilities

Break down your main job/study/after-school tasks/chores:

1. ______________________________
2. ______________________________
3. ______________________________
4. ______________________________
5. ______________________________

Part 2: The Cool and the Not-So-Cool Stuff

The Cool:
What about your job/school activities/chores do you really enjoy? Think about what makes them fun or rewarding.

1. ______________________________
2. ______________________________
3. ______________________________

The Not-So-Cool:
What do you not really enjoy? Get real about what bugs you.

1. ______________________________
2. ______________________________
3. ______________________________

Part 3: Rate Your Happiness

Take a look at your likes and dislikes. Now, imagine a sliding scale, with 1 being "Ugh, I really don't enjoy this" and 10 being "This is the best! I love it!" Where would you slide your marker?

Your Happiness Rating:

Part 4: Reflect a Bit

Based on your happiness rating, what would you say about your job/school activities/chores? Could anything improve the score?

Additional Notes

Final Wrap-Up

As you stand on the threshold of your future, remember the journey you've embarked on through these pages.

- You've explored the terrain of self-discovery, identifying your unique interests, skills, and values.
- You've navigated the complexities of career planning, setting meaningful goals that are true to who you are.
- You've gained the tools to make informed decisions about your future, empowered to chart a course that resonates with your passions and purpose.

The future might seem scary, but you're not going into it blind. You're going in with a **better understanding of yourself** and **how to handle whatever comes your way.**

Imagine having a job that makes you really happy, where you're always learning new stuff and feel like you're doing something important. Picture waking up every morning excited to get to work, knowing as well as making money you are also making your life better.

This isn't something impossible—it's something you can totally achieve. But reaching this dream takes work. It means not giving up on your goals, bouncing back when things don't go as planned, and being ready to change course if you need to. You've got to keep learning and growing, especially since the job world is always changing.

Every move you make brings you one step closer to making your career dreams come true.

As you close this book and step into the world of career possibilities, carry with you these lessons learned. Harness them as you continue to grow and evolve in your career journey. Embrace the future with an open mind, a resilient spirit, and a heart full of ambition.

The future isn't something that happens to you—it's something **you create.** And with the insights and skills you've amassed, you're well on your way to creating a career that not only fulfills your aspirations but also adds value to the world around you.

The journey doesn't end here—**it's just beginning.** It's your turn to steer the ship and find a job that makes you really happy. The world awaits your unique contributions. So go forth, armed with knowledge, courage, and an unyielding belief in yourself. Your future is yours to shape—so make it awesome.

Appendix 1
Questions that Delve into the Specifics of a Job

Here you can find some meaningful questions that look into the specifics of a job, the day-to-day tasks, the career progression, and the views on industry trends.

1. **What are the typical day-to-day responsibilities of your job?**
- Can you walk me through a typical workday or workweek in your position?
- What are the most challenging tasks you encounter? How do you manage them?

2. **Skill Application and Mastery**
- What key skills are essential for success in your job, and how did you develop them?
- How do you stay current with the necessary skills and knowledge in your field?

3. **Career Progression and Development**
- What does career advancement typically look like in this field?
- Can you describe some potential career paths one might take starting from an entry-level position in this industry?
- What advice would you give to someone just starting out in this field regarding career development?

4. Workplace Culture and Environment

- What is the work culture like in your organization or industry?
- How does your organization support your professional growth and work-life balance?

5. Industry Perspective and Trends

- What are the current trends impacting your industry, and how do you see them affecting your job?
- How might someone entering the field prepare for the future landscape of this industry?

By asking these questions, you can gain a deeper understanding of what to expect and how to prepare for a career in a specific industry or role.

Appendix 2
Your Cover Letter

Think of a cover letter as the introduction to the story of you that you send along with a request for a job shadowing opportunity or a job application.

Importance of a Cover Letter

Why can't your CV (see Appendix 4) or application speak for itself? Well, a cover letter is your voice when you can't be there in person. It gives context to your CV and can sway the employer or professional to take a chance on you. It tells them why you're the one they should be betting on and how serious you are about grasping new opportunities.

Structure and Important Elements

Most cover letters follow a simple structure:

1. **Contact Information:** At the top, list your name, address, phone number, and email, followed by the date, and then the employer's details. Just like you'd address a formal letter.

2. **Salutation or Greeting:** Start with a "Dear [Name]," If you don't know the name, "Dear Hiring Manager," works as a solid Plan B but preferably use names.

3. **Opening Paragraph:** This is where you grab attention—the most important part of the letter. Try to grab the reader's attention and make them read further. Mention the position you're applying for and drop a line or two about why you're the not-just-anyone for the job.

4. **Middle Paragraph(s):** Here you unpack your story. Link your skills and experiences to what they're looking for. Give them proof about your experiences, achievements, or projects.

5. **Closing Paragraph:** Wrap up with flair. Reaffirm your interest, and say you'd love to discuss how you can contribute to their team. Also thank them for considering you.

6. **Formal Closure:** End with a "Sincerely," or "Best regards," and your name.

Key Tips to Remember

- Tailor your cover letter for each application; cookie-cutter letters are a big no-no.
- Keep it concise—a page is plenty.
- Use a professional tone but let your personality peek through.
- Proofread! Spelling or grammar hiccups can trip you up before the starting line.

Pull one together with care, and you'll be setting the stage for success. Good luck!

Appendix 3
Personality Tests

Personality tests are like quizzes, but instead of grades, they give you a mirror reflecting bits of your inner self—your behaviors, your strengths, and how you buzz with the world around you.

Why Should You Care?

Understanding your personality can be super handy. It helps you understand why you do what you do, vibe with certain peeps, or why some activities pump you up more than others. When it comes to choosing a career path, knowing 'you' can make all the difference.

A Quick Tour of Some Personality Tests

- **Myers-Briggs Type Indicator (MBTI):** Imagine having a label that kind of sums up your personality—introvert or extrovert, thinker or feeler, and other cool combos. That's MBTI for you.

- **Big Five Personality Traits:** These five factoids—how open, conscientious, extroverted, agreeable, and stable you are—paint a pretty wide stroke of your persona.

- **DISC Assessment:** It's like the mood ring of behavior, showing how dominant, inspiring, steady, or careful you might be—especially in teams.
- **StrengthsFinder:** This one's all about highlighting your superpowers. Why be good when you can be great, right?
- **Enneagram:** Mix a bit of old-school wisdom with personality profiling, and bammm, you've got Enneagram. It's deep, a bit mystical, and could tell you heaps about your core motives.
- **Holland Code (RIASEC):** This one's like sorting hats for careers based on what floats your boat—doing, investigating, creating, helping, persuading, or organizing.
- **16 Personality Factor Questionnaire (16PF):** With16 different traits to measure, it provides great insight into your mind. Ever wondered why you're great at strategizing or why you can read a room like a book? The 16PF might just have the answers.

How Do You Use Them?

No test can define you completely. You're way more complex and awesome than any questionnaire can capture. This is just a way to begin understanding your unique qualities. You can find them with an easy search online. As you answer the tests, be as honest as you can (remember, no one's grading you), and then sit back. The results could be a convo starter, an 'aha!' moment, or just a fun thing to chat about with your friends.

So, ready to meet yourself? Go ahead, take the plunge, and enjoy. Who knows what fascinating things you'll learn about the amazing person you are. Let's get to it!

Appendix 4
Your CV

A CV is your chance to show off the awesome skills you've honed, the knowledge you've accumulated, and the potential you're zipping around with. It's the narrative of 'you' in the professional world, and sometimes it's your ticket to opportunities that can shape your future.

Structure and Must-Haves

A CV is very important. Here's what you need to include:

1. **Your Details:** Start strong with your name and contact information. We're talking email, phone number, and maybe a LinkedIn profile if you've got one.

2. **Objective or Summary:** Lead with a punchy intro about who you are and what you're aiming for. This is your "why you should care about me" spiel.

3. **Education:** Here's where you get to brag about your schooling, important courses, and those impressive grades or awards.

4. **Skills:** Shine a light on what you're good at. Maybe it's your tech wizardry, your language prowess, or even your powers of persuasion.

5. **Extracurricular Activities:** Whether you're the captain of the chess club or volunteer on weekends, it all tells the story of a well-rounded individual.

6. **Personal Projects:** Ever built a robot, started a blog, or designed a smartphone app? It's all evidence of your initiative and skill.

7. **References:** Include people who vouch for your character and work ethic (think teachers or leaders from your volunteer work).

8. **Interests:** Sometimes, those offbeat hobbies can catch an eye and help you stand out.

Your CV is a living document. It'll grow as you do with every new class, project, or extracurricular activity. Keep it updated, keep it real, and keep it you.

Appendix 5
SWOT Analysis

SWOT stands for **Strengths, Weaknesses, Opportunities,** and **Threats.** It is a simple yet powerful tool used for understanding your strengths and weaknesses while recognizing the opportunities available and potential threats you might face.

Using SWOT analysis is common in business to plan strategies and make decisions. However, it can also be used personally to help you understand your current situation, especially when making decisions about your future career.

How It Works

Strengths: These are things you're good at or advantages that you have. This could also include your skills, qualifications, talents, or positive personal characteristics. For example, being a quick learner, having great organizational skills, or being proficient at a certain software.

Weaknesses: These are areas where you might need improvement. It could be a skill you lack, an area of knowledge you're not quite sure about, or a personality trait that you're working on. For example, you might struggle with time management or find it hard speaking in public. Identifying these gives you a chance to work on them and improve.

Opportunities: These are external factors in your environment that could provide benefits for your career. These can include trends, new technologies, training programs, networking events, or career-related resources at school.

Threats: These are also external factors but these may cause trouble for your career. It could be competition from your classmates or colleagues, changes in industry which demand different skill sets, or a negative economic condition.

How to Use It

1. **Draw** a large square and divide it into four smaller squares. Label each one of the squares "Strengths", "Weaknesses", "Opportunities" and "Threats".

2. **Fill in** the boxes with relevant points. Be honest about where your strengths and weaknesses lie. Remember, the purpose of this exercise is to help you be more self-aware, and this will only happen if you are honest about where you are now.

3. Finally, **consider** all points in your SWOT analysis—how can you use your strengths and opportunities to overcome your identified weaknesses and threats? This will help you build a constructive plan to reach your career goals.

Your SWOT analysis represents **a snapshot in time,** and your strengths, weaknesses, opportunities, and threats may change over time. It's a good idea to revisit periodically and make updates as needed.

Thank You!

I hope you enjoyed this book. As an indie author, your feedback is very important to me. **If you have a moment, please consider leaving a review online.**

Your feedback not only helps me improve my content but also helps other teens and parents find the guidance they need. It's one of the simplest and most impactful ways to support my work.

If you would like to leave a review, **simply use the QR code** below:

Thank you for your support!

I hope this guide empowers you to take meaningful steps toward success.

References

Allen, David, et al. *Getting Things Done for Teens: Take Control of Your Life in a Distracting World.* New York, New York, Penguin Books, An Imprint Of Penguin Random House Llc, 2018.

Burnett, Bill, and Dave Evans. *Designing Your Life.* Knopf, September, 2016.

CareerOneStop. *Careers and Career Information—CareerOneStop.* Careeronestop.org, 2019, www.careeronestop.org

Christen, Carol. *What Color is Your Parachute? For Teens: Discover Yourself, Design Your Future, and Plan for Your... Dream Job.* S.L., Ten Speed, 2022.

Covey, Sean. *The 7 Habits of Highly Effective Teenagers.* Simon and Schuster, March, 2011.

Covey, Stephen R. *7 Habits of Highly Effective People: Powerful Lessons in Personal Change.* 1989. S.L., Simon & Schuster, 2020.

Duckworth, Angela. *Grit: The Power of Passion and Perseverance.* New York, Scribner, 2016.

Dweck, Carol S. *Mindset: The New Psychology of Success.* New York, Random House, 2006.

iMentor. *"IMentor Database."* IMentor, imentor.org

Mangleburg, Tamara F., and Juanita J. Brown. *Teens' Sources of Income: Jobs and Allowances.* Jstor.org, Taylor & Francis, Ltd., 2023, www.jstor.org/stable/40469742

MBA, MY. *Summary—Do What You Are : Discover the Perfect Career for You through the Secrets of Personality Types by Paul D. Tieger, Barbara Barron & Kelly Tieger.* MY MBA, June, 2022.

My Next Move. *What Do You Want to Do for a Living?* Mynextmove.org, 2019, www.mynextmove.org

National Career Development Association. www.ncda.org, www.ncda.org/aws/NCDA/pt/sp/home_page

National Center for O*NET Development. *O*NET Online.* Onetonline.org, U.S. Department of Labor, 2024, www.onetonline.org

Wilson, Susan B, and Michael Singer Dobson. *Goal Setting: How to Create an Action Plan and Achieve Your Goals.* New York, American Management Association, 2008.

Made in the USA
Columbia, SC
07 March 2025

54804930R00089